SELF ASHORED

Navigating Your Way on Life's Voyage

by Lenore Pearson

by Lenore Pearson

SELF ASHORED

Copyright © 2019 by Lenore Pearson

All rights reserved. Printed in Australia. No part of this book may be used or reproduced in any manner whatsoever without the written permission of the author except for the use of brief quotations embodied in critical articles and book reviews.

First Edition, 2019
ISBN 9780648493136

Indie Published by Lenore Pearson

Book Cover Design and Illustrations – Damian Cessario
What Lies Beneath Art

Praise for *SELF ASHORED*

"Lenore Pearson is not only a beautiful writer, she is a beautiful soul and her book is filled with gems of wisdom on every page. This book is unlike any other: reading it feels like sitting down to a cup of tea with an attentive and understanding friend who has been exactly where you are. There are no easy fixes or platitudes here - there is just genuine love and compassion that comes from experience. Lenore is like a wise best friend giving you a gentle nudge forward to be radically honest, compassionate and caring to yourself. This book will motivate you, heal you, and help you sail into the horizon of your best life."

—*Dallas Woodburn, Author and Writing Coach*

"In this beautifully written book, author Lenore Pearson, brilliantly invites us to experience a journey that many women tend to charter alone, a journey filled with fear, loss, depression, shame and pain. Yet, in the pages of this book, she gives us a clearly defined map to help us navigate the waters of our own emotional wounds and empowers us to become the captain; the master of our own destiny. You're going to love the action prompts and song suggestions she offers the readers at the close of each chapter. It's a perfect addition to this guidebook, after all, what's the point of going on a long personal journey, if you don't take time to self-reflect and enjoy some good tunes along the way!"

—*Char Lekx, Transformation Coach and Host of Village Mama Podcast.*

"If you're ready to look inside yourself, reflect on where you've been and what's on the horizon, this book is an impactful journey to embark upon. I recommend it for anyone who's had or having a rough time and searching for themselves. Bravo Lenore."

—*Tammi Kirkness, Life Coach, Spiritual Teacher and Founder of VisionScope Coaching*

"This book resonated with me greatly and I felt like Lenore was talking right to me or even reading my thoughts! It was a great insight into her own thought process and whilst I know Lenore professionally, this insight not only surprised me at times, but made me feel like I wish I knew her thought process when we were working together. I read this beautiful book in one sitting and, in my opinion, it will leave you feeling loved, understood and above all that you have made another friend. Loved it!"

— *Lilian Oliver, Health and Wellness Entrepreneur*

"Lenore writes from a place of genuine emotional honesty that'll have you hooked from page one. Not only are you taken on a guided exploration of your own life, but of hers as well. Like the inviting shoulder of a best friend you never knew you had, Lenore is with you every step of the way as you learn how to re-examine and re-evaluate your life for the better. Life-affirming and uplifting, this book is for anyone who is looking to say good-bye to negativity and embrace a positive and powerful way of life. It's

by Lenore Pearson

no over-exaggeration to state that this book will change your life."

— Mitchell R. Paul, Writer and Editor

"Before I read Self Ashored I found school and my studies difficult because I just didn't have a plan. This book will help you connect with the bigger picture. You will feel like Lenore is on your side and understands you on a deeper level."

— Elle Nacard, Student

Contents

Introduction   1

PART 1 - ANCHORED

Chapter 1: *Tides in the Affairs of Men*   5
Chapter 2: *Shipwrecked and Drowning*   9
Chapter 3: *Do You Give A Ship?*   16
Chapter 4: *Get Your Ship Together*   24
Chapter 5: *Moored*   31
Chapter 6: *Sailor or Captain?*   35
Chapter 7: *Seas the Day*   39

PART 2 - ADRIFT

Chapter 8: *Essential Navigation Skills*   47
Chapter 9: *Storm Trooper*   53
Chapter 10: *Unleash the Kraken*   58
Chapter 11: *Sirens*   64
Chapter 12: *Beware the Jellyfish*   71
Chapter 13: *Sharks*   77
Chapter 14: *The Rare Starfish*   83

Chapter 15: *Port of Call* — 90
Chapter 16: *Don't Keel Over* — 92
Chapter 17: *Fuel Your Ship* — 98
Chapter 18: *St. Elmo's Fire* — 104

PART 3 - ASHORE

Chapter 19: *Homecoming* — 110
Chapter 20: *Your Rowing Team* — 115
Chapter 21: *SEAcret Rituals* — 120
Chapter 22: *Ship Maintenance* — 130
Chapter 23: *Make Ship Happen* — 140
Chapter 24: *Course Correct* — 146
Chapter 25: *Ripples* — 153
Chapter 26: *Buried Treasure* — 159

Glossary of Terms — 166
The Self Ashored Playlist — 169
Recommended Resources — 171
Book Statistics — 177
Acknowledgements — 179
About the Author — 185

Dedication

For my dad John and mum Suzy, who equipped me with the strongest internal compass and the courage to raise the anchor and for Stuart, Toby, Lucas and Audrey for always allowing me to drift out on my own from time to time but giving me the best reason to come home.

by Lenore Pearson

Note on the Songs

—

While I appreciate that the songs chosen for each chapter don't float everyone's boat and in time may become outdated, they were chosen for their lyrics and how these reflect the message in each chapter. You are however, encouraged to create your own 'Soundtrack to Your Life' that resonates with the stages of your life's voyage.

Where words fail, music speaks
~ Hans Christian Andersen

"Everything can be taken from a man but one thing: the last of the human freedoms — to choose one's attitude in any given set of circumstances, to choose one's own way."

~ Viktor Frankl

by Lenore Pearson

Introduction

I am not a sailor.

I am barely a swimmer.

Put me on a boat and I get seasick. Take me to the beach and I spend my time trying to figure out ways to come home with the least amount of sand. I don't know a reef knot from a slip knot. But, if there is one thing I do know, it's that my story has been an epic voyage from the very beginning.

At times I've been aboard a luxury cruise liner with all the comfort and safety that comes with it as I've powered like a juggernaut across the ocean, stable and unsinkable. But I've also done stints in my own personal rowboat, my arms aching as I've strained to paddle against the tide all the while being lashed about by the waves. Once or twice, I've even been adrift in a tiny dinghy, totally alone, afraid and at the mercy of the ocean, wondering whether I'd ever reach land or be lost forever.

As I have encountered many beautiful starfish and the stings of a few jellyfish (more on this later) on my voyage, I've come to realise that ultimately we all have the same desired destination – a happy and fulfilled life, but the way we choose to navigate our way there can vary greatly. My story is, in many ways, no different to countless others in the world, but it's mine. Its significance is in the lessons it has taught me, some of which were learned the hard way.

I have spent a great chunk of my mental, physical and emotional health operating from what I call a 'lack mentality'. I was focussing solely on the things being taken away from my life rather than the things to be gained and it left me powerless, at the mercy of my circumstances.

There were many times I wished I could go back and correct the course my life took, avoiding the storms and replacing them with sunshine. But then my story would sound like a beautiful fairytale instead of the truly epic voyage it continues to be. It was in my lowest moments, drifting and deserted, that I realised I wasn't alone in my quest for valuable navigation skills. Many of us forget how to be the captain of our own ship.

If Christopher Columbus could accidentally discover a whole new continent and Ferdinand Magellan could circumnavigate the world, why should it be so difficult for us to navigate our own lives?

Self Ashored

Allow me to join you on your own voyage aboard the ship of life. You are the captain who steers the ship in whichever direction you choose and I am the shipmate with the map to assist you on your journey.

There will be storms.
There may even be some mythical creatures.
But there is also buried treasure waiting to be found.
You don't even need to pack; you already have everything you need.

Nothing great was ever achieved without action, without venturing out of the safety of your harbour.
But don't take my word for it, trust yourself, weigh anchor and set sail.

Oh, and of course, any great journey must include one kick-ass playlist.

ॐ **Song**: This Is Me - Keala Settle

by Lenore Pearson

Part 1: Anchored

1. to prevent or slow the drift of a ship
2. a person or thing that can be relied on for support, stability, or security

Chapter 1
Tides in the Affairs of Men

There is a tide in the affairs of men, which, taken at the flood, leads on to fortune. Omitted, all the voyage of their life is bound in shallows and in miseries. On such a full sea are we now afloat. And we must take the current when it serves, or lose our ventures.
~ William Shakespeare

Your life is a series of high and low tides. Before embarking on any great voyage, you must learn to read these tides and make the most of them. Like a ship in port that awaits the high tide to set sail, you too must keep watch to seize opportunities that will set you on the right course to success. However, if you allow the opportunity to pass or are unable to recognise it when it comes, you may become stranded at port, unable to progress. Miss too many tides or stay still for too long and your anchors will sink deeper, held fast by disappointment and resentment.

Your high tides are when everything is aligned and in flow. It is easy to embrace this time because it keeps you buoyant and your sense of purpose and stability are heightened. It becomes easier to chart a course, leave port and make way for your desired destination.

Your low tides are when you are confronted with situations that cut right to the core of your being, that bring you to your knees and make you question your reason for existing. If you don't learn to work these low tides to your advantage, they will anchor you firmly in place.

Author Andrea Dykstra said, 'In order to love who you are you cannot hate the experiences that shaped you'. Whether high or low, both tides provide perspective in your life and equally serve a purpose. There is no high tide without low tide, no happiness without sorrow and no life without death. You cannot know one without the other, just like you cannot know what you are looking for unless you have experienced the things you aren't. As difficult as they are, low tides are a necessary part of life and sometimes they can reveal hidden gems washed up on the shore that otherwise would have remained hidden.

In your low tide moments your soul is laid bare and you start to learn more about yourself, your values, your desires and the course your journey will take. It is very human of you to avoid things that cause you pain but they have the ability to show you what you may be missing and where you need to heal. Without knowing who you are and what drives you, it is all too easy for other people to create their own map for you or for the tides to bind you to a set course, perhaps one you never intended to take. The more that negative emotions get cast aside, the bigger they grow, as you lose control of them and they end up controlling you instead. It is when dealing with the anchors of sadness, anger, and grief that the best version of you is brought to life. You are like the jagged stone on the shore that is subjected to the wash of the waves. Rather than being consumed, the trials you face polish you and you are able to shine.

There is a purpose to everything you experience in life. If you open yourself up to this truth, it allows you to find peace in your circumstances. If you continue to blame situations in your life on outside forces you cannot control, you become further disconnected from who you are and the power that resides within you. Without this power you miss the high tides when they appear and have no chance of weighing the anchors of the past that bind you in place and prevent you from moving forward.

Be grateful for your low tides, but don't be so focussed on them that you miss the high tide when it comes in. Even through loss and pain, our greatest opportunities and lessons can be revealed. Peace comes when you learn to surrender to the ebbs and flows of life. They are going to happen regardless. Look at how expansive the ocean of life is in front of you, full of possibility. So many of us view this ocean through the narrow perspective of a telescope. This telescope is the lens of our past experiences. We peer through the eyepiece and our telescope focuses in on just a small part of the ocean, limiting our view. We lose that breadth of vision that allows us to see the high tides and to choose which opportunities we'll catch.

Like the gravitational force of the moon that controls the tides, something so much bigger than yourself is at play and although you feel in control at times, you cannot fight the ebbs and flows, you can only learn to navigate them. Don't give up because the tides could change at any moment. You are poised for greatness.

ॐ **Action:** Reflect and record your 'high tides' and 'low tides'. What were some of your greatest lessons during these times?

ॐ **Song:** Changing Tides - The Fray

Chapter 2
Shipwrecked and Drowning

―

Ships don't sink because of the water around them; ships sink because of the water that gets in them. Don't let what's happening around you get inside and weigh you down.
~ Unknown

Titanic: the unsinkable ship.

Boy, were they wrong!

It was "unsinkable" because of the watertight bulkheads within the ship. They weren't banking on an iceberg slicing right through numerous bulkheads, leaving a hole too extensive to withstand the amount of water flooding in from the Atlantic. It sank not because of what was around it but because it couldn't handle the magnitude of what got inside of it.

You will, without a doubt, be faced with situations in your lifetime that will test you, that will break you and that will sometimes result in shipwreck. They will leave an iceberg-sized hole inside of you, leaving you open and exposed as waves of emotion come flooding in. The waves will weigh you down and try to drown you

by Lenore Pearson

but what you need to understand is that in these moments your hardship will steer you towards where your real strength lies. You need to recognise and seize this opportunity or sinking becomes inevitable.

There is no single thing that has taught me more about life than the birth of my children. Not because it taught me how to keep them alive, but because it taught me how to keep myself alive.

My plan when I became a mum was to own it and let everyone know that I was smashing it like a pro. As it happened, the universe had other plans. From the outside, it appeared that I 'had my ship together', but this was not a reflection of what was going on inside.

I struggled through postpartum depression with all three of my children. By the time I was pregnant with my third, the inner perfectionist in me felt that I was more than prepared this time around, having been through it twice before. I knew the signs, my husband Stuart knew the signs and we both knew what help was available to us. Truth be told, I did not read the signs very well. I did not reach out as much as I should have and my depression got so bad that I probably should have been hospitalised.

Self Ashored

Guilt quickly set in for having a messy house, for ordering take-out because I was too tired to cook, for greeting my husband at the door with a screaming baby while still in my pyjamas from the morning and for not going back to work quick enough as we struggled financially.

It was when my son, eight years old at the time, said to me through tears, 'Mummy you're always angry', that the guilt turned into shame. Shame that I screamed at my baby and left her to cry in her cot, shame that I yelled at my boys for spilling milk on the lounge, shame that I threw my husband's clothes out into the hall and told him to leave because he didn't understand, shame for storming out of the house and getting in my car and driving while I was in no state to drive, shame that I fell short of who I wanted to be as a wife and mother.

The cracks began to appear by the hundreds and all it took was the wrong look, the wrong words or even the wrong song on the radio to cause me to crumble into a million pieces.

Shipwrecked.

by Lenore Pearson

I was flooded with every emotion possible, and because of the magnitude of what got inside, I was drowning.

Depression can mask itself like the iceberg that brought down the Titanic. From the surface of the ocean you only see the tip; over 90% of an iceberg sits underwater - unseen. People on the outside looking in only see the surface result of depression. They miss the other 90% of what is going on underneath. Unfortunately, people choose to see what they want to see and often don't bother to scratch the surface to dig any deeper.

My depression resulted in withdrawal and disconnection, which led to declining many social events. I didn't have the resources for other people because I didn't even have them to help myself. That was the tip of the iceberg. What people didn't see was the internal battle I was fighting. For the most part, it was delicately balanced at a stalemate, but poised for complete destruction at any moment. It astounded me how hurt people felt if I didn't go out, or pick up the phone, or if I failed to, 'just cheer up' like they suggested. I didn't want sympathy. I didn't want anyone to solve my problems for me. I just wanted someone to sit with me while I felt like I was drowning in emotion and to know when to throw me a life jacket to keep me afloat until the lifeboat came along. I wanted someone to tell me it was okay to talk about it and someone who cared enough to ask questions rather than sending a trite text message with a well-meaning emoji.

While people judged and chose to see what they wanted to see, I turned to the only choice I had left: to see things differently. It was what I learnt about myself during this time that ultimately helped me cope with the death of the one person who always threw me a life jacket - my dad.

How did I learn to see things differently? I learnt to acknowledge the pain. Don't look away and suppress it because when you turn your back on pain, this is when it catches you unprepared. It begins to weigh you down and tries to drown you. If you turn your back to the ocean, you fail to see the size of the waves headed your way and are, therefore, not prepared. If you spot a wave headed your way don't jump over it, dive into it. Face those emotions head on. And as you emerge from the wave, just keep swimming for your shore.

While you are swimming, seek comfort in people who let you acknowledge the pain. It may be that a health professional is required to help you navigate the waters you are in, to pull you off the rocks and set you afloat again. A harbour pilot is a sailor who manoeuvres

by Lenore Pearson

ships through dangerous or congested waters. For us, harbour pilots appear as life coaches, counsellors and health care practitioners - they help navigate the perilous waters because they have studied them and the hazards they contain.

For you, like it was for me, sometimes there is no immediate solution. When you can't change the outcome you need to change how you see the situation. Once you have done this, you'll notice things that you haven't before and this is when the learning and growth begins. The only way for you to fail at this is to give up. Realise there will be a great deal of discomfort in your darkest times. You will feel cold, alone and scared. But take a moment to sit with your emotions and when those cracks begin to appear, be comforted in knowing that this is how the light gets in. This is the light that shows you a different way and changes how you see the situation.

When you feel like there is no one left to fight for you, fight for yourself. This requires courage, stamina and tenacity. It is all too easy to give up, to check out of life and become a victim of your circumstances. This is as much a mental battle as it can be a physical one. To stay in the battle, find out what inspires you. Is it a powerful song? A character in a book? Your personal faith? Or a great hero of history? Once you have found a way to get motivated, take one small step forward at a time. Keep putting one foot in front of the other. Like I said to my children when they were learning to swim, 'just keep moving. Because if you stop, you sink'.

Keep a positive mindset. Stop focussing on what is wrong with you and start to recognise what is right. This will help to face the fight you have in front of you. Realise that no situation is forever and that you are stronger than you know.

You might not be thinking this far ahead, but your experience could one day be someone else's lifeboat. You might be the one to see below the surface and realise the extent of another's iceberg. You could be the one to acknowledge where someone is at in life and let them know that they are not alone. When the people you care about are shipwrecked and drowning, you will know what to do and when to throw them a life jacket.

ॐ **Action:** Make a list of what inspires you and use this when you feel like you're drowning or heading towards shipwreck.

ॐ **Song:** Feeling a Moment - Feeder

Chapter 3
Do You Give A Ship?

You are not defined by your past. You are prepared by your past.
~ Joel Osteen

Let me introduce you to a cult I have been a member of since 1980. In fact, at some point in your life you have unwittingly been a member of this cult too. It's called 'The Cult of You'.

The Cult of You ethos is to mould self-centred humans. They promote a negativity bias and operate using the following thoughts:

- I am so hard done by
- I am always taken for granted
- I do all the giving but never the receiving
- I don't care about others if they don't care about me
- I always think about everybody else
- No one cares what I do
- No one can tell me what to do

I don't know about you but I became increasingly despondent with my membership. So I escaped and haven't looked back. But let me explain how I almost became a lifetime member.

I never felt completely comfortable in my own skin. I never felt like I quite fit in anywhere. This was exacerbated by incessant teasing about what I wore or how my hair looked (the curly mullet was *totally* a trend started by me), and put-downs because I was always 'too' something - too Italian, too Catholic or too sensitive.

I didn't fit the mould or play by the rules, that is the societal rules and responsibilities that came with being raised in a culture where I was expected to carry out certain 'duties' that went against my grain. It quickly became a common joke in my family that I couldn't cook. To this day I don't understand why. Perhaps it seemed I wasn't pulling my weight because I wasn't labouring away in the kitchen cooking and cleaning at every family gathering (even though I did on many occasions but the negativity bias of others didn't allow them to remember those times).

I must have skipped over the part in the familial 'how to' manual on how to be the ideal woman because cooking was not my first passion (or second or third for that matter). I also didn't buy into the whole 'men retire to the lounge room while the women clean up' mentality. I was more of the mind, 'if you ate from it and used cutlery to do so, clean it yourself'. This could also be why my career path had nothing to do with food whatsoever.

Believe me, I was grateful for my upbringing and heritage. I was one of the lucky few who had parents I could talk openly and honestly with, parents that allowed me to shine in my own unique way while instilling solid values that I now pass on to my own children. For all my independence, Dad would jokingly call me a feminist, but secretly admired my feistiness, a quality he loved in my daughter also. I am so grateful that they allowed me to be me. And I loved being me. The one thing I was missing was how to handle the judgement, rejection and even open hostility from people who thought that I should be more like them. Doing things differently to how they had previously been done somehow always seemed to be the wrong way and apparently does not make you very favourable as a 'team player'. When you start to pick up on the tone of people's voices, the snide remarks and the exclusion you learn to be silent. You hide the colour in your life and you become a dulled version of mediocrity that everyone else approves of. They aren't going to change so you can't either.

Self Ashored

I ultimately stopped giving a ship and I paid full membership into The Cult of Me as a way of protecting myself.

As a child you are naturally egocentric, until you reach certain developmental stages where you start to acknowledge that other people exist and they have feelings too. You go along your merry way living in a perfect little bubble where you get to be yourself and have lots of friends. That is, until people start to point out that things are not so perfect and not everyone is going to like you for who you are, and the bubble bursts. When this happens it's so easy to return to your egocentric stage, where you get to make everything about you and forget about everyone else. This is full membership.

When you stop giving a ship you start to sink further and further into yourself. You become weighed down by resentment and resemble nothing but a shadow, lacking substance and emanating bad energy. If that's all you're putting out into the world, you can expect nothing but the same in return. That I can promise you.

When I became totally focussed on what people seemingly did wrong, I completely erased everything they had done right. I became an expert in negativity bias, giving more weight to the negative emotions and experiences in my life rather than the positive ones. I recalled things from the past that couldn't ever benefit me in the present and I gave myself permission to call people out on their faults the way they did with me. I wanted them to feel my wrath like Poseidon unleashing a vicious storm upon the sea. But in the end, the only person it ended up hurting was me.

I became exhausted and weighed down by the massive chip on my shoulder. I didn't feel good about myself and I projected that onto others. Not giving a ship robbed me of the joy in my life until I realised I was allowing the past to define me and shape my future. Suddenly it dawned on me that I didn't want to be one of those people who didn't give a ship. I was resorting to playing 'their' game, lowering myself to 'their' level. I was paying back negativity with more negativity.

I needed to change the rules. I needed to use my past experiences to prepare me, rather than define me. I realised I needed to be in control of my present and stop playing the victim. I needed to stop comparing myself with everyone else.

If you too want to rediscover your joy and ditch the lifetime membership to The Cult of Me then consider the following:

Stop keeping score
Not everyone is going to repay you in the same way. If your motivation behind helping people is purely the intention of what you are going to get back in return then you are going to be disappointed every single time. You miss all those opportunities for 'repayment' of different kinds. Find joy in the simple things and start opening yourself up to people rather than shutting down.

Stop relying on others to make you feel good about yourself
Don't take things personally. Other people's negativity says more about them than it does about you. Positivity has to start with you because you are the only one who is in control of your actions and how you feel.

The damage of judgement
We don't get a free ride when it comes to judgement.
What we judge in others is a reflection of what we judge in ourselves. By being harsh with someone else you are actually saying something about yourself. When making judgements of others, you are operating a zoom lens instead of a wide-angle lens. You are focussing in on one small part of that person and fail to truly understand what makes them tick. If you can get to the point where you come to know the whole person, then there's no possible room for judgement.

by Lenore Pearson

Compassion over complaining
I complained a lot about the mentality of my culture and it took me a long time to understand the meaning of compassion. When I became a parent myself I saw for the first time that those who had gone before me did the best with what they had and what was instilled in them. This is where I discovered my compassion for others. In doing so I also found permission to break the mould. I could see where others were coming from and with understanding I gained release from those expectations that were holding me back.

Always give a ship
It's ok to feel angry and hurt and check out for a little while. Just don't let yourself become resentful and get sucked into lifetime membership to the cult. Always return to giving a ship, especially about the following:
- Family (even if they don't float your boat)
- Bettering humanity
- Giving back to those who have given to you

Always be you
Live authentically, choose to show up every day and be the real you - unapologetically. As author and vulnerability advocate Brene Brown says, 'Let go of who you think you're supposed to be and be who you are'. There is only one you and your authenticity cannot be taken from you.

So rather than hiding and putting up barriers to protect yourself, set yourself free from the Cult of You. Find joy through openness. Start giving a ship about others but stop giving a ship about what you feel others think of you. In the end the most important thing is what you think of yourself.

ॐ **Action:** Write down your top 10 unique qualities. Then ask a trusted friend to write down what they think your top 10 qualities are and compare the two lists. How are you perceived by others?

ॐ **Song:** Raise Your Glass - Pink

by Lenore Pearson

Chapter 4
Get Your Ship Together

Until you're broken, you don't know what you're made of. It gives you the ability to build yourself all over again, but stronger than ever.
~ Unknown

You've been shipwrecked and broken and sunk to rock bottom. It is natural to struggle to pick up the pieces and deal with the emotions that go along with it: pain, loss, resentment. You don't feel like you can ever be the same person you once were. And you know what? You can't be and that's okay. When something has been broken and then put back together, it is never quite the same. For you, you might not shine the way you once did, but you can learn to shine in a different way, often brighter than before. You need to find the strength to become your own shipwright and rebuild your ship or you will never be able to set sail on your voyage. As daunting as it seems, rock bottom is sometimes the very best place from which to build yourself back up. When you start with a blank slate, you can be intentional about the way you put your ship back together.

Even though you are blessed with being able to build from scratch, you still need to build yourself up with the right plan and materials so you can weather the storms that come your way. You want to try to shipwreck-proof yourself as much as possible. Like building a ship, you're going to need some concrete steps to help you along the way:

Start from the bottom and work your way up
Don't look at your rock-bottom moments as a failing on your part because that's where the rebuilding starts. You can't rebuild a ship by starting with the sides or the cabin, there needs to be a solid foundation to support the rest of the ship. This foundation lies in your core values and beliefs (more on this in Part 2). When all is going well, there is no motivation to change these fundamental parts of your being. It is only when we are at our most vulnerable that we are most able to question what we believe to be true. Once we have questioned and adjusted or removed faulty beliefs we can progress to choosing the right materials.

Use the right materials
Rebuilding your ship requires you to look at what didn't quite work previously and what areas need improvement. You can't just focus on one area though; you need to look at it as a whole because everything is connected. When it comes to building yourself up you

need to consider the right materials for your mind, your body and your soul. All three are connected and when one is depleted the other two do not function to their full capacity. The right materials for you include:

Mind	*Body*	*Soul*
Personal development	Physical exercise and clean eating	Connection

Employ the right people to help you build
Sometimes you may have no choice but to build your ship on your own, but where possible seek out help from the right kinds of people. This can be one of the most challenging parts of your build. If you choose the wrong people they can slow or sabotage the construction with negativity, criticism or even downright narcissism as they make your struggle somehow all about them. With any luck, you'll recognise the wrong people quickly this time. Often, they can be the same people who were poking holes in your old ship to begin with. On the other hand, once you have questioned your core values and beliefs you are much better equipped to find the right people. They will be the perfect match for you as they share your beliefs. These are the kinds of people who are

interested in you, not because of anything they can get from you, but because you build each other up. They keep you positive, pick up the slack when you are exhausted and help you see it through right to the end, even when you feel like giving up.

Sacred space inside the ship
We all need somewhere we can retreat to when we need to recharge. This is the interior of your ship. We can become so concerned about how others see us that all we do is polish our exterior. What we say or do, what car we drive and how we look can consume our efforts, leaving a shiny exterior while our interior is rotting away from poor health, uncharitable thoughts, negative emotions and unhealthy relationships. We need to pay just as much, if not more, attention to our sacred interior. By furnishing our interior properly, we find that we have the ability to not only weather storms but also recover more quickly in their wake. Think about what you need to have in and on your ship. What helps you when times get tough? Is it finding time in your day to meditate? Do you need to arrange a regular catch-up with your best friend to debrief or maybe you need some alone time walking in nature to recharge?

by Lenore Pearson

Choose a figurehead
From as early as the 16th century, carved figureheads at the prow of a ship were commonplace. They served as powerful protective symbols for warding off evil spirits. However, you don't need to believe in spirits to make use of a figurehead's power. Once your ship has been built and you are ready to set sail, choosing a symbol or mantra of your inner strength will help protect you on your voyage. It will help you refocus on your goals when things get tough, remind you of struggles you've overcome and serve as a symbol of your inner strength, the strength you have developed to get this far. Your symbol could be anything, from a token, to an object, or even a photograph that means something to you. A mantra can be as simple as a short phrase to remind you how to overcome a struggle you are facing, or a way to prompt you to use a strategy you have developed. You might have one or two figureheads but don't have too many or they may lose their impact.

Ensure your ship is seaworthy
After ship construction but before any great voyage is untaken, there is a testing phase known as a sea trial. This is the last stage of ship building to test the vessel's capabilities at sea. When performing your own sea trial, here are some very important questions to ask yourself:

Self Ashored

What am I struggling with right now?
When am I most energised?
What am I grateful for right now?
What are my priorities right now?
What can I do for my mind today?
What can I do for my body today?
What can I do for my soul today?
What is one kind thing I can do for myself today?
What is one positive thing I can do today that is outside my comfort zone?
What is one lesson I learnt today?
What do I value in myself? What parts of my life currently align with these values?
What is one thing I could do to move forward from today?

These questions will allow you to reflect on where you are now and how prepared you are to set sail. If there is a question you are unable to answer, stop and take the time you need to think it through. This may be a minute, an hour or even a few days; only you will know when you have a suitable response.

Once your ship has been rebuilt and it is strong enough to set sail, I want you to take a step back and admire it for all its flaws. It's not the same ship you once sailed. That ship became shipwrecked because the foundations it was built on became unstable. From the outside it appeared shiny to most people, but on the inside it was rotting. Having invested the time and energy into rebuilding, your ship is standing once again but what you have in front of you is a much stronger version. You have started from rock bottom, used the right materials, found your sacred space, chosen a figurehead and run your sea trials. All that's left to do is shatter the champagne bottle against the hull and feel which way the wind blows. Don't fight it, just adjust your sails and prepare to launch.

ॐ **Action:** Answer the 12 self-reflection questions.

ॐ **Song:** Never Give Up - Sia

Chapter 5
Moored

A ship is always safe at the shore, but that is not what it is built for.
~ Albert Einstein

You have invested a great deal of time, energy, money and emotion on rebuilding your ship. You have struggled internally to carefully put the pieces back together. It has, at times, required all your strength and now you wonder whether it was all worth it. Are you even ready to launch? Ship is getting real. You think you finally feel strong enough and confident enough in yourself to set sail once again but, this time, on a very different course and this is your biggest challenge yet.

You are teetering on the edge of launching but realise that the people you thought would be on the dock to see you off are nowhere to be seen. This is the moment the past comes calling, wanting to remind you of what you're leaving behind. It makes you question your new direction, how badly you want it and what you are willing to give up to get it.

by Lenore Pearson

Your past often comes in the form of people in your life who are 'moored'. These are the people whose intentions speak louder than their actions. They are quick to tell you of their grand plans but somehow never see anything through to completion. This is why the new you scares the ship out of them. They don't know how to react to your newfound sense of purpose, energy and priorities. They don't want you to change. They can only see what they are losing – good old reliable you. It's not that they don't care or don't want what's best for you, but they haven't been privy to the process leading up to your departure; they only see the end product so their behaviour towards you may seem unsupportive. In reality, this is their way of holding on to you to maintain the status quo and keep you both safe.

The danger here is that you get entangled in their anchor chains, and end up getting stuck too, keeping you moored to the dock and taking the wind out of your sails. They don't realise that they are hurting you by feeding your self-doubt. Self-doubt is another kind of anchor that paralyses you, preventing you from setting sail. It convinces you that where you are now, in the safety of the harbour, is where you should stay because it protects you from being hurt again. Familiarity feels safe. What you don't realise is that it keeps you stuck in fear of the unknown, preventing

Self Ashored

you from venturing out and exploring other oceans. If you are consumed by your self-doubt then your life inevitably becomes a self-fulfilling prophecy. You are scared of the unknown but it is this same fear that prevents you from taking the steps needed to find out what's out there. You never have the chance to face your fears, which just increases your doubt about setting sail and leaving the harbour in the first place.

When you built your ship back up you needed to carry out a sea trial. This trial partly serves to combat your self-doubt. Use this sea trial as a smaller practice journey before you launch into a full-blown voyage. Putting yourself out there, even briefly, allows you to experience what life could be like. It shows you that moving outside the safe comfort zone of your harbour even for a moment can be liberating. It brings the colour and vibrancy back into your life. However, a word of advice, remember to take baby steps. Your test run is also there to break other people in and help them get used to the new you. Doing a complete 'one-eighty' overnight scares the ship out of people - apparently.

It requires a great deal of work on yourself before you will be ready to leave the shore but once you are poised to cast-off, expect to experience a feeling of loss. Venturing into the unknown means leaving port behind: leaving behind what is known and safe, the old you and the old way of living. This in itself is scary, but don't let it become another anchor to weigh you down. There will always be periods of readjustment, grieving and even doubts along the way. You need to have built your strategies and network of supporters and have done the work on your self-belief and courage in order to break free.

To succeed, you don't have to change your plans for others, you have to keep pushing forward and eventually those people, your anchors, will either lift and come along with you or the chains will need to be cut and they'll be left behind. This can be difficult but remember, you are not forcing them to remain behind and you can give them the chance to come with you. If you wait for everyone's approval you will never move. No one cares to invest in a ship that is stuck at shore, so invest in yourself first to enable you to weigh anchor and set sail. It will be the best investment you ever make.

ॐ **Action:** Write down the anchors that need to be lifted in order for you to move forward.

ॐ **Song:** Dare You to Move - Switchfoot

Chapter 6
Sailor or Captain?

Leaders become great not because of their power, but because of their ability to empower others.
~ John C. Maxwell

Who you are now is a result of where you have been and what you have done to get to this point. Who you become depends on what you choose to do and the person you choose to be from this point forward.

It is fair to conclude that up until a certain point in your life you were a sailor. As a child you needed guidance, structure and protection. You sailed for pleasure and gained lots of experience, but you were always part of the crew, relying on other people to tell you what to do and guide you on your current course. You have cruised along and never considered moving up the ranks.

At this time in your life other people have been in charge of you - parents, carers, teachers, employers. Someone has always been there to watch out for your wellbeing but there will come a time when you will need to step up, out-rank those above you and become the captain of your own ship.

Being a sailor isn't a bad thing, we all need to learn and grow. However, as you grow you naturally start to question what you have been taught and if the course that was plotted for you was in fact the right one. This is when it's very easy for resentment to set in. You resent your upbringing, you resent your educational institution, you resent your teachers and you resent your environment. What you need to realise is it's not realistic to expect to just step on to your ship as a captain. There needs to be a learning process where you will allow some people to take over and promote above you, but at the right time you will learn the required skills and feel confident enough to become the person you really want to be.

The main difference between a captain and a sailor really comes down to one key element - the level of responsibility. As a captain you are more aware of your environment and how it influences your course. What you learned as a sailor has been built upon and you now have the ability to tackle challenging situations with self-confidence. You are positioned to take responsibility for your own destination rather than just sailing along and expecting others to take care of it for you.

Self Ashored

As you set your sights on becoming your own captain, you will realise that you are the master of your destiny but also the master of your mistakes. Be willing to go down with your ship. A great captain will do all that they can to save their ship, or die trying. Edward John Smith was the captain of the Titanic and was history's most famous example of a captain who went down with his ship. He was widely praised for his courage and several eyewitnesses saw him return to his post on the bridge even as icy waters engulfed it. Things won't come easy on your voyage and you will have some tough calls to make, but they are your calls, your wins and your mistakes. The very best captain will learn to navigate these waters and recognise when mistakes become lessons, as they have the potential to turn you into someone better than you were before.

Never be afraid to admit fault. Sometimes you need to accept things went wrong and go down with your ship. It builds trust with those around you and will earn you their respect. Even more importantly though, this is when learning is at its greatest: when we recognise where we went wrong, figure out the solution and vow to never make that same mistake again. After all, our mistakes are rarely fatal and a great captain will always rise again from the depths to chart a new course.

by Lenore Pearson

ॐ **Action:** Decide which areas of your life you need to captain and those in which you are happy to be a sailor. Whichever areas you decide to captain, choose one aspect, no matter how small and take charge of it right now.

ॐ **Song:** Free to Be Me - Francesca Battistelli

Chapter 7
Seas the Day

Man cannot discover new oceans unless he has the courage to lose sight of the shore.
~ Andre Gide

A ship's stores are supplies carried on board to meet its daily requirements - food, water, cleaning and medical equipment. Without them, a ship and its crew will barely last a day at sea.

Like a ship, you require certain internal stores to ensure that your own daily requirements are met too. Physically, this is the food and water you need to survive. Mentally, it includes resilience and the ability to make good choices. However, emotionally, there is one essential supply that often gets overlooked - your happiness.

Many people don't realise the importance of happiness. Put simply, happiness is a way of being that helps you deal with what life throws at you. It is one of your essential provisions on your voyage. Without happiness, it is all too easy to be swamped by the next wave of challenges that comes your way. Even the most cursory search will reveal the well-established scientific benefits happiness brings to all areas of our lives.

by Lenore Pearson

Happy people are physically stronger, more productive, more confident, have more friends, find relationships easier, cope with stress better and live longer. So why wouldn't you choose to be happy?

Two of the most harmful things you can do in terms of your own happiness are:
- Setting a finish line, and
- Assigning the outcome to someone or something else.

How many times have you caught yourself saying 'I'll be happy when…'?

- I'll be happy when I have more money

- I'll be happy when I lose weight

- I'll be happy when I find my dream job

- I'll be happy when I find 'the one'

You create a sense of finality when it comes to your happiness. It becomes a destination point with a clear finish line and a very strict, black or white, yes or no, win or lose, quality. However, when you arrive, there's a shroud of disappointment when your happiness doesn't seem to be as complete or long lasting as you had imagined. You fill that void by turning to the next thing, the next finish line, not realising that reaching your finish line is like trying to catch your own shadow. It's a line that forever seems to elude you. Why? Because it keeps moving.

It has been often observed that in an age of increasing abundance, people are becoming increasingly unhappy. I feel the answer is not that people are becoming increasingly unhappy but that people are becoming misaligned with what they perceive happiness to be. They have forgotten that happiness can be 'now'. They have forgotten that happiness can be achieved with very little. Some of the poorest people living the simplest of lives are often some of the happiest people on earth. Their lives are devoid of the materialistic 'noise' that dominates our wealthy consumer culture where dollars keep the score for who is 'winning' at life.

Happiness is an internal process and you are the only one that gets to activate it. It is never determined by how many dollars are in the bank, your position at work or how many friends you have. It solely depends on you. Happiness is entirely a state of mind.

by Lenore Pearson

Your happiness is like a muscle. It needs to be exercised every day in order for it to grow and get stronger and it needs to be done S.T.A.T.

Start Taking Action Today
The only moment you have any control over is now. Begin by turning your attention from the future to the present. By focussing on where you are now, the finish line disappears altogether and your happiness becomes instant. By reframing your perception of happiness it starts to sound a little more like this:

I am grateful I have enough money to get by each day.

I am proud of who I am and I am comfortable in my own skin.

I really enjoy aspects of my job and it's a stepping-stone to bigger things.

I love meeting new people on the road to finding 'the one'.

You are the only one with the key that opens the door to your happiness. All it takes is one action and one action only - Decide Every Single Day!

One of the biggest barriers I encounter with my clients is their inability to make a decision, simply for the fact that once a decision is made it then requires action on their part to actually make things happen. And that's the hard part.

When it comes to starting something new it often involves stopping things that no longer serve you. In terms of happiness you need to:

- Stop viewing your life through the filter of your past
- Stop looking outside yourself
- Stop putting all your hope in the future

The only barrier to your happiness is YOU. If you are feeling weighed down, only you can raise that anchor. It's like taking the training wheels off a bike. At first you will feel a little unbalanced and not quite sure if you trust yourself to stay upright. But I can guarantee you the only thing scarier than lifting that anchor is staying exactly where you are.

There are three stores that are going to fuel that decision:

Passion - what lights you up? What do you always make time for? What do you naturally gravitate towards? What energizes you? Make room in your life for more of that.

Purpose - we are not born merely to exist. I truly believe that everyone, regardless of age, race, colour, ability, sexuality, financial status and marital status has a purpose to shine in their own unique way. Your passion fuels your purpose.

People - you are not responsible for the happiness of others. You can contribute to it, but you cannot own it. Just in the same way that other people are not responsible for your's. No one owns your happiness other than you. No one can walk your path for you but you most certainly don't have to do it alone. Your passion and purpose will then fuel your connection to other people - the right people: the people in the ship *building* business, not the ship demolition business and the ones who lift you up, not tear you down.

Now that you have decided, you've cleared the decks of the thinking that does not serve you; you've loaded the stores of Passion, Purpose and People that you need, what next?

You need to get started. If not now, when?

Self Ashored

Lao Tzu said, 'A journey of a thousand miles begins with a single step'. You need to take that first step and then just concentrate on where you will tread next. Keep the vision of your goal in mind, but don't let it distract you from where your next step needs to take you.

Which brings us back to realising that your future is now. It is what you do in the present that determines what tomorrow looks like. It is time to lift that anchor that has been weighing you down; you have a whole ocean of possibility in front of you. Even if you feel like you might be heading in the wrong direction, you need to get moving. Your course can be corrected, but no one ever reached a destination by staying exactly where they were. You need to stop playing small and stop bobbing up and down at the mercy of the tide, never heading anywhere. Play big, dream big dreams, take charge of your happiness and seas the day. Choose to be cast adrift and trust wherever the wind takes you.

ॐ **Action:** Revisit the anchors you wrote down in Chapter 5. Commit to lifting one that has been weighing you down.

ॐ **Song:** Brand New Day - Alex Lloyd

by Lenore Pearson

Part 2: Adrift

1. floating without control; drifting; not anchored

Chapter 8
Essential Navigation Skills

It is not the ship so much as the skilful sailing that assures the prosperous voyage.
~ George William Curtis

For the spontaneous and vivacious souls such as myself (read: often impulsive, jump now and ask questions later type), unfortunately setting sail is not as easy as jumping out of bed one morning, deciding to buy a boat and off you go. Just like a skilled captain, there are particular navigation skills that are required to give yourself the best chance of reaching your destination:

- Know where you are at any given moment
- Plot a course
- Know which way to steer to best reach your destination.
- Stay calm
- Learn how to tie a knot
- Look for the lighthouse
- Always know where the rum is stored

These navigation skills can't be assumed. Just because you are living your life as the captain of your own ship, does not mean you know where you're going or how to confront challenges and dangers along the way. The old sea dogs, the experienced and hardened captains, were always regarded with great respect for the knowledge they possessed about navigating the 'seven seas'. This was the hard-won knowledge and wisdom gained through firsthand experience of being adrift, marooned, lost and tossed to and fro at the mercy of the ocean.

You will see how these essential navigation skills can be applied to your own life. You will learn to use them to build your resilience through this next part of your voyage. If you are challenged to look for a different perspective while you are adrift or lashed by a storm, you can rely on what you have learnt. Subsequent chapters detail steps you can take to put your new skills into practice and guide you onward to the destination you choose.

Know where you are at any given moment
Before setting out it is important to check in with yourself to ascertain where you are now, where you are going and what you will need to get there. You possess an internal GPS: that part of you that directs you in which way to go, when to make a detour or when to turn back and start again. Like a GPS in a car, it relies on frequent updates with best routes and traffic alerts

so you can be informed ahead of time to determine the best direction to drive in. It's the same for your internal GPS; you need to check in with it every single day in the form of a self-awareness check.

You will learn: how to be self-aware.

Plot a course
Life should have its spontaneous moments, but you can't just drift endlessly in the hopes of eventually reaching your destination. If you are determined to arrive somewhere worthwhile, you need to plot a course. Once your internal GPS has located your current position, begin with setting a vision then work on a plan. Think big and then come back and work out the steps you need to take to get there. Even the best laid out plans need to make allowances for detours and ports of call along the way. If you don't have direction you will be easily thrown off course. If you don't know where you're going, how will you know if you arrive?

You will learn: to have direction.

Know which way to steer to best reach your destination
My husband was a boy scout and the Boys Scout's motto is, 'Be prepared'. Inevitably you are going to meet with unfavourable characters and circumstances

on your voyage. Don't be disheartened if you get thrown off course, you will be ready with the skills you need to gently guide you back. If you spend too long heading in the wrong direction, it will take so much more of your time and energy to correct your heading. To avoid this, some forward planning is what's needed.

You will learn: how to be prepared for unfavourable circumstances.

Stay calm
I don't know about you, but if I'm in a heightened state of panic and someone tells me to calm down, I want to poke their eyes out. Panicking never serves anyone, least of all the person doing the panicking, so in order to avoid a situation where someone may get a black eye, you need to ask one question, 'Can I help this situation?' If you can't control it, worrying is futile; if you can control it then there is no cause for worry. If you are cast adrift on your own, you need to remain level-headed, think clearly, ask for help and start making plans to tackle your immediate problem. However, you need to look out for your inner critic who is poised to rock your boat.

You will learn: to manage your inner critic.

Learn how to tie a knot
Former U.S. president Franklin D. Roosevelt once said, 'When you reach the end of your rope, tie a knot in it and hang on'. Some of you will reach the end of your rope quicker than others. There will be times where you will want to quit. When it feels like nothing is going right and the easiest option is to just give up, find something to hold on to. Look at how far you have come along that rope and be grateful for your biggest challenges because they will reveal your biggest lessons. Learn to tie a knot, hang on and swing into action.

You will learn: how to have gratitude for your biggest challenges.

Look for the lighthouse
A lighthouse is a stoic structure of safety, guiding the way forward through rough waters. When adversity hits like a tsunami, the lighthouse is your way through the darkness. It may present itself as a visual sign or a person or a feeling. No matter how it manifests itself, your lighthouse is powered by your intuition. Knowing what, when and who to trust is vital in weathering rough waters.

You will learn: how to trust your intuition.

by Lenore Pearson

Always know where the rum is stored
If all else fails, pour yourself a drink, stand at the stern of your ship, salute the sun and look forward to a brighter tomorrow. Life keeps moving on. This is sometimes the greatest comfort when things get tough.

You will learn: to let go of what you can't control.

ॐ **Action**: List all the survival skills you already possess that you can rely on to get you through life. Are there other skills you would like to work on?

ॐ **Song**: How Far I'll Go - Alessia Cara

Chapter 9
Storm Trooper

We must never forget that we may also find meaning in life even when confronted with a hopeless situation...When we are no longer able to change a situation, we are challenged to change ourselves.
~ Viktor Frankl

Voyages of any length come with the inherent risk of the weather turning. At some point there will be the imminent threat of bad weather. When a ship is faced with a storm there can only be two ways to proceed: to sail around it or sail through it. If it is too dangerous to proceed through the storm, a wise captain will choose a different course. However, not every storm can be avoided. Sometimes the safest place for a ship to be during a storm is out at sea because it is a safe distance from anything it could crash into. But the captain still needs to take control and steer the ship through the storm rather than letting it get thrashed about by the waves and to prevent it from taking on too much water.

by Lenore Pearson

The Latin writer Publilius Syrus observed that anyone can steer a ship when the sea is calm. What makes the best captain, however, is one who has been through a lot of storms. A ship is well equipped to withstand a storm at sea, but how well equipped are we when faced with our own personal storms?

Buddhist philosophy recognises *Three Universal Truths*, one of which is that everything is impermanent and changing. In life there is no darker storm or more significant symbol of impermanence than losing someone you love.

Death is the epitome of a hopeless situation. Sometimes though, the tragedy of death lies not in losing a loved one but in losing yourself in the chaos of the storm. In these moments, you can allow your situation to define you and control your destination. Often, it is not death itself that you fear but continuing to live when your loved ones are gone. By attaching yourself to impermanent things you can't help but fear that one day they will be gone. You need to learn to face your fears and understand that impermanence is teaching you to let go.

Loss changes a person. Life as you know it is never the same and a great deal of energy is spent blaming people or situations that could not be controlled no matter how determined you are. This is your fear of impermanence at work, and this is what it was like for me. When I lost my dad I came face to face with my biggest fear. In a split second the impermanence of life revealed itself and while the mother of all storms approached, I realised there was no avoiding the storm I had to weather. This was where I had a choice - to allow the tidal wave of emotion to wipe me out or transform tragedy into triumph.

How you steer yourself to enter your storm will determine how you exit it. Storms test your willpower and reveal your sea legs: your ability to adapt and stay balanced. Storms will most certainly come, they will stir things up and attempt to throw you off course but like the experienced captain, it's all in how you navigate your way through it that counts.

Just like physical storms, your metaphorical storms are hard to predict and even harder to control. When you can't control the situation you can still control how you respond to it. Human history is marked by those who have weathered some of the biggest storms imaginable; people such as Malala Yousafzai, Bethany Hamilton and Nelson Mandela all turned their tragedy into triumph. Others like Viktor Frankl, an Austrian Holocaust survivor, left maps for us to navigate by in penning his best-selling book *Man's Search for Meaning*,

by Lenore Pearson

with the indispensable message that in life you can't avoid suffering but you can find meaning in it.

The truth is you never lose yourself in your storms if you keep your eye on your destination. Instead, you become lost when you stop trusting yourself. In these moments you can get knocked down once or twice; your ego gets bruised because you realise you are not invincible and you are not exempt from making mistakes or failing. Just like the experienced captain who has weathered his storms, it is only after the knocks, mistakes, failings and resultant bruised ego that you are better equipped to chart a course in a better direction.

Ultimately, a storm is never permanent. It approaches, it wreaks havoc but then it diminishes and it never lasts forever. Whether you choose to sail around your storm or sail through it, the most powerful measure of triumph is how you emerge from it. Stand in your storm, look for the lesson and be a storm trooper.

She stood in the storm, and when the wind did not blow her way, she adjusted her sails.
~ Elizabeth Edwards

Self Ashored

ॐ **Action:** Reflect on a storm you have weathered successfully. What was the lesson?

ॐ **Song:** Dancing in the Storm - Boom Crash Opera

Chapter 10
Unleash the Kraken

She was powerful, not because she wasn't scared but because she went on so strongly, despite the fear.
~ Atticus

When I was asked to consider writing this book, for a whole week afterwards I could think of nothing but all the positive ripples it was going to create by being shared with the world. But when it came time to sit in front of my computer and start typing, the only word that came to mind was the 'F' word.

Fear.

Who am I to write this book?
What if no one buys it?
What if I get judged?
What am I going to write that hasn't already been written about?
What the hell am I going to wear to my book launch????

Writing this book was like standing naked in front of the world.

Self Ashored

I kept it secret from most people for fear of being judged, or in case someone said something unsupportive. I know only too well from previous experience that once you have decided to untether yourself from the anchors that weigh you down, you need to be alert for dangers lurking in the deep. Have the courage to set sail and find your place in the world but be prepared to be tested. Nothing tests you more than fear.

Fear is an emotional response to something you perceive as a threat. It can be anticipating a sudden attack on an unwitting character in a scary movie. It can be fretting about how to pay an unexpected bill that arrived in the mail. It could be thinking about how you would cope if you lost someone you loved. It can also be the realisation that you might actually reach your goal, and then what? How do you keep that fire burning?

Feeling fear is a natural human response, but learning to control it and have it serve you rather than control you, can be a near impossible task. Our relationship with fear can be likened to coming face to face with the kraken. The kraken is a mythical sea monster that was believed to swallow ships whole and create huge waves, even tsunamis, to swamp ships as it trawled the oceans.

by Lenore Pearson

Like the kraken, fear has the ability to grip us with its wretched icy tentacles and prevent us from moving forward, as its hulking shadow looms over us waiting to swamp our ship and pull us under.

But like the kraken, fear isn't real.

It lives inside you, lurking in the depths of your mind. Not existing in the present moment but manifesting in an imagined future where your fear is unfounded. It is a primitive function of the human brain designed to protect you with the 'fight or flight' response. It can be a healthy response to keep you alert in tricky or unfamiliar situations, but if it is triggered every time the phone rings, or when a bill arrives in the mail, you have allowed it to swallow you whole. Fear has a place on your voyage but you need to consider what part it gets to play.

Much like the captains who have weathered the storms and gained a healthy respect for the dangers of the ocean, you need to have a healthy respect for the role that fear plays for you. You need to manage your fear by recognising it as it takes form and put in place strategies to keep it in perspective. It may have a small role to play in keeping you safe but it does not get to determine the outcome of your journey.

I like to think of fear as the universe's way of creating equilibrium. Once you have decided to free yourself from the anchors that weigh you down and set sail to find your place in the world, you will find life will start working for you. But in a moment, your fortunes can change. The universe sets in motion the mythical beasts from the deep, the waves and tsunamis in order to keep you honest. It tests you to see if you really want to reach your goal, to see if it is worth the risk.

When I hit a lull in 'book-creating' momentum it was because my mythical beast emerged from the darkness in the form of opinions - other people's as well as my own. People will always have something to say. I have sat around tables while people have been torn to shreds over their life decisions, all the while sitting and listening to what was not said. I have come to understand that this is a reaction to other people's fears and the limits it imposes upon them. People will often berate the very things they are fearful of doing themselves.

It is important to understand and identify your fears so you can learn to move through them with courage and conviction. Our biggest growth happens outside our comfort zone, so a little bit of fear is a clear signal you're in the right place. Your voyage takes shape when you venture beyond that zone into the unknown and have faith that you have what it takes to face the next challenge.

How much did I want to write this book? Was it worth the criticism and judgement?

One. Hundred. Percent.

Why? Because my reason for doing this far outweighed any reason for not doing it. I needed to work out why I wanted to write this book. You might be surprised to learn my reason for writing was me. I needed to explore, process and lay out all the lessons learnt in my journey to date. My hope was that if I could save just one person from that same kind of heartache I felt, then it would have been worth it.

Having courage is not being fearless; it's having fear and carrying on despite it. When you look fear in the face it can change the way you view your life and the way you respond to each and every challenge. It puts the wind back in your sails and helps chart your course through calmer waters.

Climatic moments of fear on your voyage will either signal the gradual sinking of your ship as it succumbs to the kraken or you'll accept the challenge and fight back. Either way, you are the one in control of your fate.

ॐ **Action**: Identify your fears and recognise what is holding you back from overcoming them.

ॐ **Song**: Fight Song - Rachel Platten

Chapter 11
Sirens

If you can't love yourself, how in the hell you gonna love somebody else?
~ RuPaul

Hollywood movies could be made from the stories I have created in my head. And I'm not talking romance or adventure movies either. My stories would fit nicely into the psychological thriller genre where elements of mystery, drama, action and paranoia are intricately intertwined with a distorted sense of reality, leading to the execution of a series of regrettable events.

This type of storytelling is not born of creativity; it is born of pure fear generated from the inner critic that inhabits the dark corners of your mind and waits like a predator for the perfect moment to launch an attack when you are most vulnerable.

Your inner critic is a Siren. According to the ancient nautical legends, the Sirens were believed to lure sailors with their enchanting voices and lead them to their eventual demise. Your Siren is your own self-critical voice that will usurp the captaincy of your ship,

Self Ashored

throw you off course and steer you towards the rocks. The Siren's call is seductive. However, in order to avoid almost certain shipwreck, you need to take charge by changing the conversation you have with yourself.

Your thoughts are powerful. They create your sense of reality, so what you tell yourself matters. They can keep you imprisoned and control your words and actions or they can liberate and elevate you to a completely different way of living. Succumbing to your Siren is like being in a bad relationship with yourself: seductive but destructive.

In modern life we are becoming more aware of what we feed our body but how conscious are we of what we are feeding our mind? If you're like most people, you have unknowingly created a lifelong habit of thinking negatively about yourself by not managing your inner Siren. Whatever you feed your mind is what will manifest within it. It's the Law of Attraction: negative will attract negative and positive will attract positive. It is so much easier to believe in the negative than the positive. The more you are seduced by your Siren the more you start to believe the lie rather than the truth. And what's worse is when you start to listen to and internalise other people's voices too. It's like having another critic inside your head. Pretty soon it will feel like you're standing in a room full of people yelling over the top of each other, as the crescendo eventually drowns out your own voice.

This is exactly what it is like to live in my head sometimes!

I am coasting along, feeling like I am on the right track and then the Siren calls. The fear, the doubt and the self-sabotaging thoughts appear. If only you could have climbed inside my head while I wrote this book. It would have scared the hell out of you. It sure scared the hell out of me!

The more you allow the negativity to take over, the more your internal dialogue will affect your external dialogue. I have sat in rooms with people where their inner Siren is expressed in how they speak to people. They feel powerful in the moment tearing others down with negativity but all it shows is how internally unhappy they are.

Your negative thoughts are generated by your subconscious mind. However, it is difficult to change this pattern of thinking. As a safeguard, your mind is equipped with a risk assessment tool. When you try to feed your subconscious a new way of thinking, it will kick in like an antivirus program on your computer. It will send out messages to alert you to an unknown threat that does not compute. It works to reject this new way of thinking. So how can you take control?

Begin to quarantine.

During the Black Death plague all ships were required to be isolated before any passengers could go ashore to prevent the disease from spreading. In much the same way, your thoughts may be powerful but you can control them. You need to quarantine your negative thoughts and find a way to delete them altogether so they don't spread.

Here are some of the best ways to do this:
- *Remove 'always' and 'never' from your vocabulary* - these words are extremes and absolutes. In the same way that these words can hurt relationships with other people, they can hurt your relationship with yourself as well.
- *Stop predicting the future* - your crystal ball is an illusion; the only moment you should ever worry about is the present because it is the only moment you have control over.
- *Don't mind read* - what you think of yourself is bad enough, what's worse is believing you know what other people think of you. You waste so much time, energy and emotion over-thinking what people might say and do. You are

better served putting that energy into having the difficult conversation itself, rather than trying to get inside the minds of others. Ask people what they meant or how they feel; more often than not you have made up a completely different story in your head.

- *Befriend your inner Siren and give it a name* - mine is Robin - after the late and very talented Robin Williams. The voices in my head sound something like the montage of voices Robin Williams creates in *Mrs. Doubtfire*. By giving your inner Siren a name you take away its power because it ceases to be your voice.
- *Affirmations* - the quickest and easiest way to rewire the subconscious mind is through consistent repetition of short positive statements beginning with, 'I am'. Repeating this statement at least twenty times a day out loud begins to strengthen the neural pathways in the brain, helping to start the shift from negative thinking to positive. My favourite affirmation is, 'I am a badass warrior!'
- *Meditation* - I love seeing the look on people's faces when I tell them I am a meditation therapist. 'She's one of THOSE people,' they seem to say. The only barrier to meditation is other people's preconceived ideas about it. I

have experienced firsthand the benefits meditation has had on my own inner Siren.

Things to keep in mind with meditation are:
- The goal is not to have an empty or silent mind, it's to have control over what the mind thinks about. This means not thinking about anything outside the present moment.
- It is for everyone. There are literally hundreds of different meditation styles and there is a style to suit everyone. It's just a matter of finding the one that works for you.
- You can't do it wrong; it just takes practice. Begin with five minutes a day and build from there.
- It needs to be one of your non-negotiables – eat, drink, sleep, wash, meditate.

Think about all the hurtful and unhelpful things you say to yourself. Now picture the person you love the most standing in front of you and you saying those words to them. Does it sit well with you? If it doesn't feel right saying it to someone you love, why would you say it to the person that matters most - yourself? When you start to change the conversation you have with your inner Siren you become more powerful than your thoughts.

by Lenore Pearson

Love and respect yourself first.

You are powerful.

You are worth the risk

Start believing it.

ॐ **Action:** Listen to how you talk to yourself and every time you catch yourself saying something negative, I want you to write it down and then write a positive version next to it.

ॐ **Song:** Going Under - Evanescence

Chapter 12
Beware the Jellyfish

Should you find yourself the victim of other people's bitterness, ignorance, smallness or insecurities, remember things could be worse. You could be one of them!
~ Unknown

Have you ever observed the graceful movements of a jellyfish? They are rather beautiful to watch, seemingly minding their own business as they freely swim around, unbeknownst to surrounding prey that their trailing tentacles are armed with stinging cells waiting for the perfect victim. The tentacles release venom that subdues and paralyses their target. Whilst the target of their prey is other marine life, they can also injure humans. What seems like a harmonious sea creature is actually a cleverly disguised predator.

These predators also move amongst the human genus.

If you have watched the movie *Bridget Jones: The Edge of Reason*, you may recall a scene where she is out socialising with her friends when they suddenly alert her to a 'jellyfisher' approaching. Bridget is in her blissful bubble of love with Mr. Darcy, or so it seems,

by Lenore Pearson

until she is stung repeatedly by the words of this 'jellyfisher', rendering her speechless.

I crack a smile every time I watch this scene because it is so easily relatable. Jellyfish are the people in your life that, on the surface, appear to be beautiful and harmonious but have hidden tentacles lurking close by. Like the marine creatures, you are attracted to them for various reasons but beware the stingers! They wait for the right moment to sting you with their words or actions, leaving you paralysed and powerless.

Their tentacles tend to appear in one of two situations - at the height of your success or at your most vulnerable moment. The catalyst for a jellyfish deploying these tentacles is feeling threatened. It is purely a defence mechanism.

Like any feeling human, our first instinct is to sting back. I have had whole conversations in my head about how to bring jellyfish down a peg. Trust me when I tell you that is exactly where those words should stay, in your head, because they never have the desired effect when said out loud. When negativity comes knocking at your door, never invite it in for a chat. This is a difficult lesson in self control, but if you learn to master the art of compassion and understanding I guarantee you will win at the game of life; not defeating the jellyfish at their own game but by changing the game altogether! There is a beautiful quote that says, 'A rising tide lifts all boats'. These jellyfish are navigating their own voyage in the best way they know, with what resources and understanding they have. But when you rise above their stings and bring positivity into the situation, you can lift them in the process. This, in turn, has its own intangible rewards.

Just by looking at a jellyfish there is no way to tell that it is made up of 98% water, has no brain or heart and that its tentacles are armed with powerful venom. It is what we perceive that determines our impression of a jellyfish. We have no idea what lies below the surface. Sadly, we often treat humans in the same way. We look at the surface of a person's life and make assumptions, but seldom do we take the time to dive deeper to understand their journey or what drives them to be the way they are. It is like looking only at the surface of the ocean and not fathoming its expansive depths.

What if I said that you actually need jellyfish in your life? I would go as far as to say they are essential to your growth. Handled with care, they are the people that can fuel that fire in your belly; they are the ones that motivate you and push you to greater heights. We need to be challenged to achieve our best. The trick is learning how to minimise the stings along the way.

by Lenore Pearson

To treat a jellyfish sting is a three-step process. You need to pour vinegar on it, remove the tentacles and apply heat. The good news is, this same three-step process can be used for human jellyfish too.

How to treat human jellyfish

Step 1 - Neutralise their poison by pouring positivity onto the situation. In other words, use their stings to motivate you to keep going so you can prove them wrong. Figure out what you can learn from the experience.

Step 2 - Remove the tentacles by keeping them at arm's length. Some jellyfish might be people you can't avoid but you can certainly work on not letting their tentacles get a hold of you. Manage the amount of time you spend with them and be selective about the situations in which this happens.

Step 3 - Apply heat by being fabulous. Burn so bright that they don't have the power to dampen your success.

After the initial shock of a sting, make some space for reflection and gratitude. This is a powerful preventative tool. As we continue on our journey through life our survival instincts are hardwired to

Self Ashored

remember the stings. Unfortunately, we seldom remember the complimentary things said to us. Be assured, jellyfish are not a threat to you. What they say is a reflection of where they are on their journey, not a projection of where you should be on yours. You are their reminder that they are not out living a life they love. The more you are confident in who you are and living a life authentic to you, the less other people's words will be able to affect you.

Once you know how to handle the stings, you can take control of the situation. This is the moment when you stop being on the defensive and the relationship becomes easier. You now have an opportunity to help them grow. It is by breaking down barriers between you and the jellyfish that the long term affects of a sting will lose its intensity. The jellyfish may begin to see you as less of a threat and more of an ally. Remember that there was something that initially attracted you to this jellyfish, or that there was a reason you found yourself in the same part of the ocean together. Remind yourself of that every time the stingers appear. You hold the power; use it to help them grow.

By rising above the negativity, you help others to rise with you.

by Lenore Pearson

ॐ **Action:** Identify your jellyfish and make a point of getting to know them on a deeper level.

ॐ **Song:** Titanium - David Guetta feat. Sia

Chapter 13
Sharks

I think that I am familiar with the fact that you are going to ignore this particular problem until it swims up and BITES YOU ON THE ASS!
~ Matt Hooper (Jaws)

American surfing superstar Bethany Hamilton has a remarkable story. At thirteen years of age, Bethany lost her left arm to a 14-foot tiger shark while out surfing with friends. As a rising star in the surfing community, it appeared her career was over. Yet, she returned to the water one month after the attack and went on to win a national title two years later. She became 'Unstoppable'. She taught herself to surf with one arm, continued competing, became a wife and mum and went on to inspire countless others. The point is not that she survived a shark attack; it is that she fought back and reclaimed who she was despite it.

We all have our sharks to deal with. Rarely, though, are our sharks the same as the ocean predator in Bethany's story. Instead, your sharks are the people that contribute to the toxicity levels in your life. These people are toxic and one-sided, and they could be friends or you might even be in a relationship with them. When your sharks attack, they don't have rows of teeth to chew you up, rather they suck the life out of you. They take more than they give and you end up becoming less than who you were meant to be. They have the ability to consume all that is good and meaningful inside of you, leaving behind a shell of the vibrant and energetic person you used to be. You feel drained, lack confidence in yourself, feel oddly dependent on the shark in your life and feel trapped, perhaps out of obligation or guilt, and unable to move on.

Now don't get me wrong. Where possible I try to see the best qualities in people before I judge their worst qualities. I like to give a chance or even two. But sadly, sometimes, some people are just not worth it. Their negativity and thoughtlessness are a poison.

If you are concerned there may be sharks circling you, here are some traits to watch out for:

15 Shark Traits

- *Blame* - blame never falls onto them. It is always everyone else's problem, never their own.
- *Negativity* - it's a disease. The more they project it, the more it spreads.

- *Manipulation* – it's their way or no way. Gifted with manipulating a situation to best suit them without any disregard for how it affects other people.
- *Judgement* - often judges other people on the exact qualities they themselves possess. Very quick to make up their mind about someone without actually taking the time to get to know them or their situation.
- *Critical* - strips you bare. They go to town on all your flaws and have no remorse for doing so. A little bit of success is like blood in the water for sharks. They wait for the perfect moment and then go in for the kill.
- *Uncaring, unsupportive or disinterested* - these are the people that never ask. They know full well what you're up to, and they are the first to tell you that they know what you're going through, but they have never actually been interested enough to ask. They say they are supportive but you have never actually heard a supportive word come from their mouth.
- *Unapologetic* - the word 'sorry' is not part of their vocabulary basically because they are never wrong.
- *Irresponsible* - there is always an excuse defending their poor behaviour.

- *Pathologically lie* - anything to prevent the truth from coming back to bite them on the ass.
- *Ultimatums* - they will always make you choose.
- *Abusive and rude* - this doesn't even deserve an explanation.
- *Talk more than they listen* - their story is always way better than yours; they are only concerned with themselves.
- *Drama central* - they seem to gain power and importance by being the hub of all things. They love to be the reporters of the latest gossip and thrive on other people's drama.
- *Disappointing* - they never come to the party. They are consistent in being inconsistent by always letting you down when you need them the most.
- *Jealous* - their silence in your greatest triumph is jealousy at its grandest.

I think I speak for every person that has ever watched the movie *Jaws* when I say that as soon as you step foot in the ocean you can't help but hear the theme music play in your head. In the movie it was a warning sign that the shark was approaching, looking for its next tasty victim. In life, sometimes you may be in a situation where you are neck deep in water and you can't see the impending shadow of a shark on the attack. This is when you need 'shark spotters' to sound the warning bells. These are the people in your life that always watch your back. When you are so consumed by someone or something and the water gets turbulent, it gets difficult to see. Without your spotters it is not until the shark 'swims up and bites you on the ass' that you realise you're in danger. If you find yourself in this predicament you need to be prepared with shark attack survival skills.

How to survive a shark attack

- *Go for the eyes or gills* - detect the weak spot and you may have a chance. The shark will see you are a credible threat. While I'm not suggesting you resort to physical attacks, sometimes you may need to fight back in some way. You need to avoid being the victim and take positive steps to regain your power.
- *Stand your ground* - going vertical in the water is always the best response to make a shark keep its distance from you. This means you need to be confident and assertive. Don't be afraid to be blunt with them sometimes.
- *Reduce angles of attack* - form strong, positive friendships so the sharks can see you have backup and so you can quickly identify toxic relationships.

- ***Stay out of their habitat*** - shark infested waters. Avoid situations where sharks will be. Minimise your exposure. Make an appearance then make your excuses and leave.
- ***Shark nets*** - set boundaries for the sharks.

In the end you need to have perspective. Sharks aren't necessarily bad people, they are just not the right people for you. They don't add any value to your life and as such there is no need to open your life to them. It's okay to cut ties if they don't serve you. There are plenty of other fish in the sea!

However, don't let your fear of them prevent you from enjoying the ocean. Bethany Hamilton got back in the water because her passion for surfing was greater than her fear of sharks. Your passion and will to live a fulfilling life should far outweigh the shark attacks you have endured. But know when to swim away. When you are free from the grips of their jaws, you can find your flippers and learn to swim on your own.

ॐ **Action:** Identify the sharks in your life and take steps to survive an attack.

ॐ **Song:** Roar - Katy Perry

Chapter 14
The Rare Starfish

Your soul mate is not someone that comes into your life peacefully. It is who comes to make you question things, who changes your reality, somebody that marks a before and after in your life. It is not the human being everyone has idealized, but an ordinary person, who manages to revolutionize your world in a second.
~ Unknown

On a family holiday in Fiji, while floating in the still and shallow ocean water, I was in awe of how many starfish there were: blue, red, pink, purple, some fully visible and some hidden beneath the sand barely making out a star shape. Hoping to find a rare nine-armed sea star, I was apprehensive to put my feet down for fear of stepping on one. Had the water been constantly moving and choppy, I would have totally missed the impact of these radiant sea creatures. Unlike jellyfish that are a little showier and in constant movement, starfish are unassuming and steadfast. They can appear when you least expect them and yet their beauty and impact can be felt for years to come.

by Lenore Pearson

Rare starfish can appear on our life's voyage too. They are those impactful people and moments in your life that clearly define a before and after. You can't miss them, although in the moment you are sometimes transfixed by them, it is only afterwards you begin to see their significance. You just need to be open to recognising them.

Seeing starfish can be a reminder to slow down. Just like the water, I needed to be still to see the starfish with clarity. In life you also need to slow down. Open your eyes to see and your ears to listen; everyone has a story, every experience has a lesson. It is through these stories and experiences that the rare starfish present themselves.

I had one such moment at the horse races.

It was a freezing day in Melbourne for a girl's weekend away. Dolled up in our best race frocks and huddled down one end of a long table enjoying the endlessly flowing glasses of champagne and orange juice, we came to know two fun-loving guys called Scotty and Mark. As the day went on there was the sharing of fashion tips and the best horses to back but there was also the sharing of life stories.

Self Ashored

In my lifetime, I have heard many stories of where people have come from and what has brought them to this particular point in their life but none have impacted me the way Scotty's story did.

Every day in the news we are bombarded with sensationalist journalism, dramatically reporting lucky escapes, heroic deeds and tragic loss but until you have heard one of these stories first hand, the impact and gravity of the event is not the same.

Scotty was one of four men to have survived a tragic plane crash, one of Tasmania's worst aviation disasters. At 21 years of age, bulletproof, with a promising footy career and a tribe of men he considered family, Scotty, along with his teammates, set off on three charted flights to Launceston for an end of season trip. Scotty's plane was carrying ten passengers. As it came in to land it hit power lines, taking off the left wing, transferring all the weight to the right side and bursting into flames on impact. Every passenger on the right side of the plane perished.

Scotty was sitting on the left.

He lost six of his best mates that night and the road to recovery was a long and challenging one. With full thickness burns to 33% of his body, pressure garments

by Lenore Pearson

and stockings became Scotty's armour for the next two and a half years.

People like Scotty are rare starfish. The jellyfish may sting, the sharks may bite but the starfish can regenerate. They lose an arm but they can grow one back. Scotty may not have lost an arm but he regenerated in other ways. How could anyone move on from something like this?

They continue to live.

For Scotty it started with his very own rare starfish. Scotty's dad told him to keep going and just get on with it. We recognise today that his was a way of thinking from the past generation. A generation raised in a post-war world that learnt from their own fathers that life was precious and that those left behind had to somehow pick up the pieces and carry on. They had hope and positivity for a better future and grit and determination born from genuine hardship.

In the darkest days of World War Two, Winston Churchill famously said, 'If you're going through hell, keep going'. In this way, Scotty's dad helped him realise he couldn't wait to feel better to start living again; he had to live first and believe that the healing would come. Having practiced martial arts since he was eight, Scotty had already developed a fierce sense of self-discipline. This allowed him to take a firm hold of his father's advice and foster a growth mindset that played a key role in his rehabilitation.

Scotty's other great strength was that he wasn't afraid to ask for help. He made sure that he saw a counsellor who helped him process his survivor's guilt and come to terms with the question, 'Why them and not me?'

I can't begin to tell you how many times on my voyage I wanted to pack it all in, give up, and disappear. I spent a good part of my life trying to control as many things as I could after discovering a lot of things I couldn't. For me, Scotty's story was a reality check. I had drifted for far too long, so long in fact that I lost touch with life. I had let fear steer my boat. If Scotty could take some brave steps forward to work with the reality of his fear, pain and recovery instead of letting it consume him, then I really had no excuse tackling the comparatively insignificant hurdles in my own life.

Keep watch for the starfish in your life. In recognising them, you acknowledge the aid they have given you when you needed it most. Your rare starfish could be a teacher that left an impression on you, a grandparent who gave you a different perspective on how life should be lived, or even the person behind you in the

by Lenore Pearson

grocery store who paid for a packet of cheese you had to leave behind because you ran out of money (it really happened to me). Then again, it may not even be a person. It could be the lyrics to a song you heard at a significant moment, a book you read or even an artwork that has revolutionised the way you look at your life. In recognising your starfish, you magnify their effect on your life allowing you to be more intentional in how you navigate life's rough seas.

Never underestimate the power you have within you to make an impact. Right now you might be reading this thinking you have nothing to contribute. You are focusing on what you don't have, on the 'missing limbs' of your life and not focussing on the fact that you can regenerate them. What is to stop you from being the rare starfish in someone else's story?

I was a primary school teacher for five years. Compared to the lifelong careers of other teachers I have known, I never thought that five years was enough to make any impact on a child's life. That was until I received an email ten years later from a former student, now at university finishing off a teaching degree, who felt moved to share with me that I was the person who inspired her to become a teacher. Had she not taken the time to let me know, I would still to this day be wondering if I ever made a difference. Thank you Marina, I am honoured to have been your starfish.

You have everything within you to be someone else's rare starfish. Go and teach them how to live.

ॐ **Action**: Record the names of your rare starfish and the impact they have had on your life, then go one step further and write a letter of gratitude (that's right, pen and paper) and let them know how they impacted your life.

ॐ **Song:** Change Your Life - Little Mix

by Lenore Pearson

Chapter 15
Port of Call

It's ok if you fall down and lose your spark. Just make sure that when you get back up, you rise as the whole damn fire.
~ *Colette Werden*

When a ship's stores are depleted the ship will struggle to carry on its voyage unless those stores are replenished. You too will have moments on your voyage in which you have powered on while your internal stores have been diminishing. When the engine of the ship is chugging and your spark is faltering, you may have no other choice but to find a port of call in order to gather provisions for the rest of the journey.

A port of call will consist of a time when you need to take a break from your journey and focus on yourself and your wellbeing. However, once you have disembarked, it is all too easy to stay on shore and abandon ship forever.

It is ok to disembark and disconnect, it is ok to check out and retreat and it is ok to catch your breath and build your energy. It's actually important to do so. All you need to do is to find a port of call that suits you.

When you return to the ship, ready to weigh anchor once again, you'll be prepared to tackle the next stage of your journey, well supplied, re-energised and, sometimes, even with a new direction, stronger than ever before.

But it should only be a short stint.... kind of like this chapter!

ॐ **Action**: Write a list of things you can do when you need some time out. Pick one and do it right now.

ॐ **Song**: The Great Escape - Pink

Chapter 16
Don't Keel Over

To succeed in life you need three things: a wishbone, a backbone and a funny bone.
~ Reba McEntire

The keel of a ship is a structural beam that runs right down the middle, from bow to stern. The significance of this beam is that it gives greater stability and rights the ship when it tips to bring it back to its centre. You could say it's the backbone of the ship.

To be able to sail through life you need to have a backbone. Physically, it provides you with the stability to sit, stand, run or walk. Your backbone is also a symbol of strength, belief and commitment to confidently and proudly know who you are and what you stand for.

One of the best ways you can strengthen your backbone is to identify your core values. Your core values are your moral compass; they point you in the right direction, especially when decisions need to be made. They help you make more sense out of life. They are guiding you whether you realise it or not.

It is likely that many of you reading this have never consciously considered what your values are, let alone written them down somewhere. If you find that you are unsatisfied in your career, you never seem to be happy and settled in a relationship or you always manage to attract the wrong type of people into your life, it could be because you have never taken the time to understand and get clear on what makes you you.

You want to avoid situations where you 'keel over'. This happens when a ship tilts so far to one side that it can't recover and therefore capsizes. In life, this may be a situation where you find yourself operating so far from your values that it causes serious tension and damage in your life. You find yourself no longer living an authentic life that fulfils and energises you, but instead you are drowning in dissatisfaction, pain and emptiness.

Should you find yourself drifting off course or unsure where to turn next, you need to check in with your values, the backbone of your ship, your keel: the only part that can set you right again. The best chance you can give yourself at sticking to the right course is to identify your values, check in with them consistently and re-evaluate them when necessary.

by Lenore Pearson

Identify your values

There are extensive lists of words to describe values that you can find online (I love a good Google search) but there are hundreds to choose from. How many values should you have? Is there a perfect number? Reading through these lists can become stressful and it is so easy to wonder if you are choosing the 'right' values. Choosing from a list of words can almost be like a shopping expedition when you're hungry, all these wonderful empowering words jump out at you and rather than choosing what defines you best, you end up choosing values you wish you had or think you should have. Truth be told, there are no 'right' values, only values that are right for you. Ideally, you only need a handful to work with, just a selection of a few words that describe what you stand for. The best way to identify your core values is to reflect on past experiences and ask yourself the following questions:

- What are the most important things in my life right now? E.g. family, friends, career
- What is most meaningful to me? E.g. travel, being creative
- When am I at my happiest? E.g. when you dance, sing, workout
- When have I felt most fulfilled? E.g. when you spend quality time with family, helping others

Then get very clear on why these are so important to you. Once you have a list of values written down, pick your top 5 and list them in order of importance.

Check in
Your values are tested most when you need to make a decision. Choices that are aligned with your values tend to feel right and can highlight the wrong choices in a similar way. Ultimately, checking-in helps to realign your ship, stay on course and be true to who you are. When it comes to life changing decisions in particular, don't be afraid to put everything on hold while you check in with your values. If saying yes to this decision is aligned with one or all of your values then jump in with both feet. However, if you can't tick off at least one value then it's a clear sign that it may be the wrong choice at this point in time.

Re-evaluate
When you identify your values, they are not set in stone. Over time your life changes, you change and as such, your values will change too. For example, one of my values was relationships with other people. While this is still very important, my studies in this area and the mammoth amount of personal development I have done helped me realise that I needed to focus on my relationship with myself first before I could make any positive changes in my relationships with other people.

by Lenore Pearson

I was never going to be any use to anyone else if I couldn't value and respect who I was first. Which is why it is important to make a commitment, at least once a year, to re-evaluate your values. This is a great substitute for the dubious practice of making New Year's resolutions. I would also recommend identifying at least one value that never changes, the one value that defines you through and through that you would never compromise on. For me, it is authenticity. It is my number one value and regardless of where I am headed, who comes in and out of my life, what job I have, or how much money is in my bank account, I will never compromise on who I am. Everything I do is with that in mind and whether other people are comfortable with who I am is never the question. Whether *I* am comfortable with who I am is always the question.

My husband's favourite quote from author Mel Thomson is, 'If you don't stand for something you stand for nothing'. It takes courage to remain true to your values and be the only one saying 'no' when everyone else is saying 'yes'. But this is the exact quality that boosts your credibility and trust, even with those who disagree with you. And, more importantly, it allows you to live without regret, knowing that you spoke up for what you believed to be important and used your moral compass to do what you know to be right.

ॐ **Action:** Identify your top five core values, in order of importance, then write them down and circle the one that is unlikely to ever change.

ॐ **Song:** I Don't Want to Be - Gavin DeGraw

Chapter 17
Fuel Your Ship

Should you find yourself in a chronically leaking boat, energy devoted to changing vessels is likely to be more productive than energy devoted to patching leaks.
~ Warren Buffett

It is easy to be aware of your physical energy. You very quickly realise when you are exhausted, run down and need to rest. Similarly, you feel energised when you are taking care of your physical body through nutrition and exercise. However, this is different from the energy your soul possesses. You often hear about people who have presence, those who are inspiring or those who light up a room. This is to do with their soul-energy, which is so much more than what they feel in their physical body.

Despite your best efforts to stay on course, ship will happen. There will be moments when other people or events will drag you down and deplete your soul-energy stores; stripping away part of what makes you shine. But what does this do to your energy levels?

Your energy is a big part of your outward presence; it speaks before you do. When you function from low, negative and fearful energy, your world and those around you begin to react to you in much the same way. But on the other hand, when you function from high, positive and hopeful energy, your world and those around you become positive and hopeful too. You will attract what you focus your energy on the most - the positive or the negative. By changing your energy, you change your life and potentially the lives of others. Your energy is more powerful than you could ever imagine, mainly because it is transferable and absorbable. So you need to be vigilant in how it is distributed.

Bunkering is the supplying of fuel for use by ships, loading it and distributing it among available bunker tanks. This is exactly how you should view your own energy. Steps need to be taken to refuel your energy and distribute it accordingly, but when doing this, I highly recommend you have a protection policy in place.

Strategies for refuelling and protecting your energy

- *Awareness* - notice how you feel when you're in the company of certain people, notice how you react to particular topics of conversation and pay attention to your surroundings and what this does to your energy.

- *Breathing* - when you are aware of a negative change to your energy, breathe. This not only promotes peace and calmness but it also halts the fight or flight response in its tracks, avoiding potentially draining reactions.
- *Grounding* - this is the practice of absorbing the earth's natural energy through direct contact with the earth. It's as simple as stepping outside barefoot. Feel the grass on your toes and reconnect to your place in creation. It's a great way to bring you back to reality and get you away from your perceived stresses, thoughts and beliefs.
- *Mantra/Affirmation* - one of the best ways to dispel negative thought patterns is to repeat a mantra or affirmation such as, 'I listen to my body, it knows exactly what I need' or 'I attract positive energy by radiating positive energy'. The words we say to ourselves can have a huge impact on our thoughts and beliefs.
- *Visualise* - this was one of the best strategies my own coach gave to me: to visualise a bubble of light surrounding and protecting me before I entered a room where I knew there was potential for energy drainage. Use your car for this as you travel to a stressful meeting or your

daily work and visualise a white bubble of light protecting you, so any negativity that floats your way can be deflected.
- *Crystals* - if you are partial to the healing power of crystals, then seek out those that help to ward off negative energy. My black tourmaline bracelet is a go-to for me whenever I know I may be in the presence of negative energy flow. Even if you aren't into crystals, a meaningful object can be a great token to remind you to allow negative energy to bounce right off you.
- *Sanctuary* - dedicate a place, either in your home or away from home, where you can refuel your energy on your own. A sanctuary helps you bring calm and peace back into your life and to surround yourself with the things that inspire and energise you.
- *Boundaries* - vampires really exist, well energy vampires anyway. They will suck you dry so it is essential that you set boundaries. Begin with social media. Now, let's get one thing straight, social media is not damaging, it's the way some people use it and how you interpret those messages that is damaging. Do a social media detox once in a while, disconnect and when you have refuelled, selectively choose what platform you are going to give attention to, or if it doesn't serve you in any way, disconnect for good. You

might also consider selectively blocking some contacts!
- *Distance* - give yourself permission to step right back from potentially draining situations. This may very well be a difficult task, in particular if it's a social occasion (especially where family are concerned), or even an aspect of your work that you find taxing. Fortunately, you can control how much of your time and energy you give to different parts of your life. For example, as much as you would do anything for family, it does not give them the right to drain you of your resources. If they do, there will be no back up energy supply for when you need it the most, and particularly when they need you the most. With your relationships it is often much easier and more energy efficient to jump ship rather than fix something that isn't serving you. Be cautious in doing this because there are respectful and honourable ways of creating distance without cutting people from your life for good.

Negativity has the potential to be one of the greatest drains on your energy. How many times have you started your day feeling great, only to have someone take the wind out of your sails? As much as we don't want other people's negative beliefs and energy to affect us, it can be a real challenge to prevent it from doing so. The good news is that negativity can only affect you if you are on the same frequency as it, so change the station, change the song and retune your receiver back into positive channels. The minute you have one ounce of belief that any particular negativity might be true or real, you begin to buy into it and give it the power to grow until it saps all your strength.

You are responsible for your energy. Radiate the kind of energy that lights up a room when you walk in, not when you walk out. Don't spend it trying to change people who don't want to be changed, shift your energy in a different direction altogether. Use it for the good of humankind, because the more people in this world that operate from positive energy, the better the world will be.

ॐ **Action:** Develop your own energy protection policy. Name the people and situations you'll use different strategies with. What new strategies can you come up with?

ॐ **Song:** Suddenly I See - KT Tunstall

by Lenore Pearson

Chapter 18
St. Elmo's Fire

I stopped waiting for the light at the end of the tunnel and lit that bitch up myself.
~ Unknown

There comes a time on your voyage when a moment of clarity signals to you that it may be time to head back to shore. This is what I like to refer to as a St Elmo's moment.

During stormy weather at sea, there is a phenomenon that is said to occur towards the end of a thunderstorm during times of high static electricity. Sailors describe it as a luminous glow coming from the top of a ship's mast, which appears to be on fire but doesn't burn. This natural occurrence is known as St. Elmo's fire. Traditionally, sailors believe this to be a good omen from St. Elmo, the patron saint of sailors, signalling the end of a storm and bringing comfort and reassurance that land was ahead.

This omen was a visual sign that assured sailors that they were headed in the right direction. They couldn't see land ahead but they trusted the omen nonetheless. Unlike sailors, our St. Elmo's moments won't necessarily be as clear as a beacon of light. Such a moment is more likely to manifest itself as a fire in your belly to make a change. This is your intuition. Intuition is a knowing without reasoning. It is literally a gut reaction.

One of my most powerful St. Elmo's moments came at one of my darkest times. For a year after the passing of my dad, I felt the need to power on. I was fuelled by adrenaline and a lust for taking control of as many situations as possible for fear of more bad things happening. This did not serve me in any way, shape or form and it resulted in me distancing myself from many people and ultimately falling into an emotional mess on the floor of my hallway after yelling at my husband and children to get out of the house. Sitting on the floor for what seemed like an eternity, paralysed as a year's worth of tears and anger were released, I was afraid. I felt alone and rather than feeling able to take control of my situation, I felt powerless. But it became a crossroads in my journey.

I was faced with two choices, as I scrolled through the contacts in my phone for someone to call and realised there was not one person with whom I felt brave enough to verbalise what was going through my head in that moment. It was a choice between going to my medicine cabinet and deciding which cocktail of pills

by Lenore Pearson

was going to eradicate the pain, or to summon up whatever strength I had left to pick myself up off the floor and take the first step in moving forward. I chose the latter.

I had ventured off course for quite some time. I had looked for the answers externally, trying to control my situation, but I ignored the answers that came from within. Hitting rock bottom was the catalyst for remapping my voyage; it was at rock bottom that I could hear my intuition at its clearest. I sat and kept company with every feeling and emotion that washed over me in those fifteen minutes on the floor, until in the silence one stuck. To this day I can't tell you exactly what propelled me to pick myself up off the floor, but trusting my intuition made me feel alive again.

How do you learn to trust your intuition?

Be slow and silent
If you have journeyed for a while and battled a few storms, be assured that signs come across your path as a way of telling you that someone or something is watching out for your greater good. Slow down. Sit in silence. Listen. If you rush the journey and constantly live for the future or dwell in the past, you miss the opportunity to tune into what these signs are telling you.

Self Ashored

Know what sets your soul on fire

What did you love to do as a kid? What did you want to be when you grew up? Was there someone you aspired to be like? Reclaim that childhood sense of wonder where limitations and self-doubt didn't exist. That fire in your belly is guiding you to a keener sense of what you want. It is when you're fired up about something that you are more open to the signs around you pointing you in the right direction.

Trust your gut

Would you believe your gut is really the boss? Your gut produces more feel good hormones than your brain. If something doesn't feel right or, on the other hand, an exciting prospect creates butterflies in your belly, don't ignore it. Intentionally engage your brain's reasoning to take another look at the situation.

Stop waiting for the external signs. Instead, bring awareness to the internal ones. When you have been thrown off course, your intuition has the power to realign you. After being thrashed about by the waves, witnessed the storms, treated the jellyfish stings, fought off the sharks, clashed with the Sirens and found the rare starfish, you have drifted long enough. The reason you are being guided in a certain direction may not be logical or even evident straight away but that is what trusting your intuition is all about. Your potential sits much higher than where you have been operating from. You have gained some life experience; you have learnt what it means to have faith and trust, not in other people, but in yourself. Intuition is the gentle nudge signalling to you that now is the time to come back and put into practice all you have learned. It's time to return to shore.

But don't be surprised if your arrival is at a different destination to your departure.

ॐ **Action**: Sit in silence and practice connecting with your intuition following the steps above.

ॐ **Song**: St. Elmo's Fire (Man in Motion) - John Parr

Self Ashored

Part 3: Ashore

1. on the shore; on land rather than at sea

by Lenore Pearson

Chapter 19
Homecoming

---

*It's a funny thing coming home. Nothing changes.
Everything looks the same, feels the same, even smells the
same. You realize what's changed, is you.*
~ Eric Roth

You are born into this world with a radiant soul, the very essence of who you are. But as you travel through life and are faced with unpleasant experiences or trauma, it feels as if little pieces of your soul break away dulling your radiance and inhibiting your ability to shine. In the Shamanic healing tradition, this is explained as soul loss and can be viewed as a protection mechanism as you begin to discard the parts of your life that are too painful to deal with or accept. These may be parts of yourself that you don't like, losing someone you love or fighting with those closest to you. Your life then becomes fragmented and you begin to feel worn down, lost and incomplete.

Like putting the pieces of a jigsaw puzzle back together, a soul is not complete without all the pieces back where they belong. While you are fragmented, you will realise that your soul has been yearning for something more. You may find you have been searching outside of yourself, trying to fill the missing pieces with meaning from the world around you: a new car, money or the perfect relationship with your dream partner. Instead you need to look within. This requires thinking and puzzling it out, trying new ways of fitting the pieces, and of course, some strength and resolve. Those missing pieces of you remain discarded until you feel strong enough to call them back to make your soul whole again. I love this idea that you and your soul can never truly be lost, no matter what challenges you have faced. Instead, your pieces are merely out of place and that it is up to you to decide when and how you are going to bring those pieces back together.

Mark Twain famously wrote, 'The two most important days in your life are the day you were born and the day you find out why'. As you start to discover your own 'why', you will begin to see more clearly how you need to fit back together, piece by piece. Your soul is the part of you that drives you to be all that you want to be, so as the pieces return, you are more able to see yourself clearly. Everything you have learnt and endured on your voyage has led you to this point, your homecoming. Take advantage of what you have learned and use it to fuel your strength and resolve as you bring your pieces back together.

by Lenore Pearson

You will never feel completely ready for your homecoming because there is still so much to learn about life and about yourself, but it is important to take the first step and do your absolute best with what you have at this point. Take all those incredible emotions and experiences, the pleasant and unpleasant and use them to empower you to examine who you are and realise where those pieces ought to go.

You will know you are ready to come home when you begin to feel comfortable in your own skin. You have begun the inner work you need to start finding the right place for those discarded pieces. As a result, you can comfortably and rationally deal with all those emotions on a very different level. You will once again feel complete, because you have come home to yourself.

Being at home in yourself is where you feel calm and centred. It requires you to let go of who you think you're supposed to be and embrace who you are right now in this moment.

Don't let perfectionism and expectation mess with your homecoming. Growth and change is rarely neat and rarely perfect. The truth is it's often painful, messy and perfectly imperfect. It is unrealistic to assume that as you pull into the dock those nearest and dearest to you will be there to welcome you with open and accepting arms. You are not returning to the same point you departed from, so expect that things will not remain the same. Things around you may not have changed but you certainly have. Don't forget you are in a process of becoming new and whole again. You are not coming home for other people; you are coming home for yourself.

Do not base your self-worth on other people's perceptions of you, real or imagined, for this will only interfere with your homecoming. Part of loving and accepting who you are is letting go of what other people think of you. You cannot rebuild your soul when you are relying on others to help find or even substitute for those discarded pieces.

Be aware that the Sirens will resurface during this process and attempt to lure you back to a false sense of security. They will try to trick you into believing that your change is not worth the risk and it would be much easier for everyone if you just remained at sea, lost and incomplete. To combat their alluring call, change the conversation with yourself into one of positivity and then slowly change the conversation with other people so that they begin to know and understand the new you.

by Lenore Pearson

You will come back and you will SHINE! You will radiate exactly what you expect to receive from the world so do it with determination and conviction. If it ever gets to a point where others want you to dim your light because they can't handle the brightness, then take motivational speaker Lisa Nichols's advice and hand them a pair of shades. Nobody gets to dim your light unless you let them.

Come home, but never arrive! You are a living, breathing, learning being. Always be a work in progress.

ॐ **Action:** Decide what you want and invest in a Vision Board to start planning what you want to attract into your life.

ॐ **Song:** Pure Shores - All Saints

Chapter 20
Your Rowing Team

Lots of people want to ride with you in the limo, but what you want is someone who will take the bus with you when the limo breaks down.
~ Oprah Winfrey

My view of friendship was once very different.

In my 20s friendship was easy. I mixed with lots of people, I enjoyed meeting new people and I could party till four in the morning. My friends were people to spend time and share fun experiences with. I didn't need their help, because there was nothing to worry about - life was pretty simple and straightforward. I used to think that my worth was determined by the number of friends I had. In nautical terms, I had a cruise ship full of friends where it was party central. Life was literally 'cruisy'.

A cruise ship full of people is energising - everyone on board is taken care of and having fun, but are these the people you really want around when you have to abandon ship in a rowboat? Are they going to pick up an oar when you can't go on or throw you a lifejacket when you're overboard and drowning?

A few of them will. These few are what I call your rowing team.

These are the people who know your heart, who 'get you' and love you just as you are. They challenge you to be the best possible version of yourself and cheer the loudest when you are winning and are there to lift you up when you're not. These are the people who feed your soul. They are the team inside your tiny boat who keep pulling on the oars when you feel like giving up; they are the ones that make sure you reach the shore safely.

Motivational speaker Jim Rohn famously claims that you are the average of the five people you spend the most time with. These are the people closest to you that have the greatest impact on your life. Just think about that for a second. Who are the people you spend the most time with? What qualities do they possess? What values do they have? More importantly how do you feel when you are in their company? Do they deserve a place in your rowing team?

It is a life changing moment when you start to notice the people you spend the most time with. You may find that you are holding on to relationships that no longer serve you. You may have accidentally allowed some 'cruisers' on your boat. Sure they might sporadically and reluctantly pick up the oars from time to time but their lack of commitment will ultimately weigh the boat down.

This doesn't mean you throw them overboard and bid them farewell, it just means their influence has now become dead weight. While they're still on your boat, make room for them, but don't rely on them to keep you moving forward.

Inevitably this comes with its own form of grieving. It certainly did for me. After I got married, became a mum and life got trickier to navigate, I realised a lot of my friends wanted to stay behind on the party ship, while I paddled on alone. Life had become a bit more real. It wasn't cruisy anymore and it meant letting go of people who weren't prepared to paddle along with me.

I began to understand that while being surrounded by lots of friends is a wonderful thing, as life changes, it's the quality of those friendships that matter the most, not the quantity. I no longer needed a cruise ship full of friends to validate my worth; I just needed a few committed rowers.

by Lenore Pearson

From all the cruisers of your youth, how do you know who the rowers are? Reflecting on the process of finding my own rowing team, here are three simple ways to ensure you have a solid one:

Know yourself first
If you don't know who you are first, you won't know the kinds of people you are looking for. Know what your values are, what you value about yourself and what you value about your life and this should be mirrored in the right people. This helps you become very clear on who you are and who you are not and who adds value to your life and who doesn't. First you must know who you are on your own, so you can then know who you are as part of your rowing team.

Be open to new people
Push your own personal boundaries; get out of your comfort zone because this allows you to be open to new people and new experiences. Expand your social circle. Join a fitness group. Learn something new. Join online communities of people with similar interests. If you can't find the right group then be brave enough to start your own, as it is highly likely other people are looking for what you have to offer. All of this opens you up to connection with the right kinds of people.

Release judgement

One very important lesson in finding your rowing team is that judgment can't play a part. Judgment closes you down and narrows your view of others. As a mum, I naturally gravitated towards other mums because we had something in common, which *was* important, but I also found that people without kids brought just as much value to my life. They kept things real in a different way and have proven to be some of my strongest rowers.

Don't be quick to judge what other people can bring to your life and to your rowing team. Some people will row for a short period of time and hop out of the boat and some will be committed rowers. Don't be disheartened if your team changes. It just means that space opens up for another rower. And always remember that to find the right friends, you need to be the right friend.

ॐ **Action:** Identify the people you spend most time with then select five of them you want as part of your rowing team. List their names and next to each write a word or two about what they bring to your crew.

ॐ **Song:** Stand by You - Rachel Platten

by Lenore Pearson

Chapter 21
SEAcret Rituals

A daily ritual is a way of saying, 'I'm voting for myself.'
~ Mariel Hemingway

If you were to look up the definition of ritual in the dictionary it would say something like, 'a religious or solemn ceremony that is performed according to a fixed order'. Every culture has its own sacred rituals that are performed in honour of a particular person or event: Burns Night in Scotland (in honour of Scottish poet Robert Burns), flag throwing in Tuscany, the Cooper's Hill Cheese-Rolling and Wake in England, jumping seven waves on New Year's in Brazil and the Day of the Dead in Mexico, to name a few.

Similarly, there are rituals that are a part of nautical culture - a boat naming ceremony, breaking a bottle of champagne over the bow to launch a new boat and marking a sailor's first crossing of the equator with a line-crossing ceremony.

However, have you ever considered rituals in the culture of you?

Self Ashored

You do things everyday that you would likely consider part of your daily routine, but the word routine can suggest things you do on autopilot, or without noticing. This is why I prefer to use the term ritual, which conjures up a much more mindful approach to what you are doing and how it makes you feel. A ritual has deep meaning, it is sacred and involves a particular way of doing things that creates a special moment. It is a way of 'voting for yourself' every day. On your voyage of life and especially after your homecoming, it is necessary to establish some rituals that are essential and significant to the culture of you. Your rituals are an easy way to add something into your day to look forward to. I have three particular rituals that I stick to on a daily and weekly basis:

- Morning ritual
- Evening ritual
- Sunday blues ritual

Morning ritual
There is a saying, 'If you win the morning you win the day'; meaning how you start your morning will impact the rest of your day. I believe everyone is a morning person, just at different times of the morning, so regardless of when your morning begins, make it count. My morning ritual involves the following: sitting out in the sun with a cup of tea while listening to one of

my favourite podcasts. I then do a Loving Kindness meditation (refer to recommended resources), followed by 20 minutes of yoga while burning incense or diffusing essential oils, then and only then do I tackle emails and work for the day. Granted this does not always happen, some mornings don't go according to plan, however when it does, I guarantee my day is more productive and less stressful and my husband and children have the added bonus of coming home to a more even-keeled wife and mother. This whole ritual is relatively quick and easy and requires very little preparation or even cost.

Evening ritual
I adore my evening ritual. Regardless of the type of day I've had, an evening ritual is an essential and meaningful part of my day. It gives me something to look forward to when I get home but it also allows me to reflect and accept, reflecting on how my day evolved and accepting it for all its rewards and challenges. My evening ritual always consists of a cup of herbal tea and either sitting and watching one of my favourite shows with a couple of squares of dark chocolate or lighting a candle and sitting in bed with an uplifting book and filling in a page of my gratitude journal. I can then confidently let my head hit the pillow without analysing or overthinking what happened throughout my day. Never underestimate the power of finishing

your day well. Your balanced and relaxed self will sleep more deeply and restfully, preparing yourself well for the day to come.

Sunday blues ritual
Sundays with the family are such a beautiful time but it always seems to be tinged with a little sadness and anxiousness at the thought of Monday approaching. To overcome this little cloud that seems to hover on a Sunday afternoon, I implemented the Sunday blues ritual. Any preparation for the week ahead needs to be done by 3pm. I then run a bath, with Epsom salts (more on this shortly), light a candle, set up my little Bluetooth speaker and play the Late Night Jazz playlist on Spotify, grab a wellbeing magazine or book and depending on the day or week I have had, there may or may not be a glass of pink moscato involved. This resets my body and mind and sets me up for a positive start to the week.

In his book *Uncertainty*, Jonathan Fields addresses the practice of establishing 'certainty anchors'. These are something known and reliable in your life that acts as a grounding experience, that you can turn to no matter what is going on in your day. Daily rituals act as certainty anchors, especially when you are feeling anxious and off balance. When establishing your own rituals, consider the pillars of intellect, spirit, emotion,

by Lenore Pearson

movement and connection. Having an element of each is a wonderful way of creating a holistic approach to your rituals.

Before I got married, had my family and basically became a semi-responsible adult, taking care of myself would involve classy dinners and drinks with friends, weekends away, trips interstate, a shopping frenzy or even splurging on some nice frilly underwear (sorry Stu, that doesn't happen anymore). Not that I would turn my nose up to any of this if it was a viable option but taking care of yourself does not have to involve lots of money, if any at all. I came to learn many ways of ritualising my day that made it meaningful without it costing me money I didn't have. These rituals quickly became a non-negotiable part of my day.

Here is a list of inexpensive ways to take care of yourself:

Daily
- *Tea ceremony* - I'm very grateful to my mum for introducing me to the world of tea. The whole process of brewing a cup of loose leaf tea has become a very meaningful ritual. The Japanese have a whole ceremony that honours the tea making process. It is so much more than boiling a kettle and steeping a tea bag. There is

something about using loose leaf tea and a proper teapot that gives you permission to slow down and enjoy the process, either on your own or in company. As my mum always says, there is no problem a cup of tea can't fix.
- *Essential oils and candles* - there are many healing and therapeutic benefits to diffusing oils (100% pure essential oils). Depending on the oil, it can help promote relaxation, relieve tension and clear the mind. Lighting candles (as natural as possible) for soft ambient light before bed is preferable over light from a device or other bedroom lighting as it helps to promote sleep.
- *Music* - create a 'soundtrack of your life'. Music helps regulate thoughts and emotions. Creating your own personal playlist can influence how you feel throughout your day. This is your go-to playlist for when you need to give life a little kick up the ass. It motivates and inspires you. If you could put your life to music, what songs would you add?
- *Journaling* - spoil yourself a little and buy an inspiring journal that will encourage you to take some time in the morning and evening to record your thoughts and emotions. This assists in training your brain to focus on the positive aspects of your day through gratitude and intentional actions and counteracts negative

thought patterns. It is a wonderful way to organise your thoughts and record all the positive things in your day, so you can refer back to them on the not so good days.
- *Personal care* - both men and women can benefit from ritualising their whole personal care routine of a morning or evening. Buy good quality products (as natural and chemical-free as possible) that your body will thank you for. Enjoy the process of feeding your skin (or freeing it of unwanted hair). Look into the amazing benefits of dry skin brushing and remember that what you put on your body is just as important as what you put in your body!
- *Cook a beautiful meal* - I don't *love* cooking but being a little more mindful of what I eat and trying a new cuisine makes the process a ritual rather than a chore.

Weekly
- *Watch* - your favourite movie, TV show or inspiring documentary.
- *Indulge* - in some quality dark chocolate.
- *Catch up with a friend* - if you want to take care of yourself, be aware of who you spend time with. You want this to be the kind of person that leaves you feeling like you've had a day at the spa - relaxed, re-centred and rejuvenated.

- *Vitamin sea (the healing ocean)* - ideally, immerse yourself in ocean water but the next best thing would be to treat yourself to a salt bath. Grab a bag of Epsom salts and add a cup or two to your bath. If you want to heighten the experience, I highly recommend adding a few drops of your favourite essential oils: lavender and rose are divine. Soak until you feel relaxed and grounded. This particular combination helps to draw out toxins, lower stress hormones and help balance pH levels.
- *Visit your happy place* - find a place that is just yours that you can walk to or visit. Somewhere you can reflect, journal or just sit in nature.

Once a year
Okay, so some of these will involve some dollars but for once a year, you are totally worth it.

- *Have an affair* - with yourself. When was the last time, if ever, that you took yourself away for a night, weekend, week? Where would you like to escape to on your own just to reconnect with yourself?
- *Take yourself on a first date* - if you don't know what you like, how will you know who best to connect with? Ask yourself all the necessary questions:

- Favourite colour?
- Favourite food?
- Favourite holiday destination?
- What makes you laugh?
- *Day spa/retreat* - have a total day of bliss where someone else gets to take care of your wellbeing for a few hours. This is when a day of indulgence delivers a range of health benefits. Disconnect, unwind and treat yourself to a good massage, facial and sauna and yes men, you can do this too!
- *Create a belief statement* - in an earlier chapter, I discussed the importance of identifying your values. Creating a belief statement is putting all these values into a statement that reflects what you wholeheartedly believe about yourself and about your life. The more authentically you live your life, the less energy it takes. Type it up, print it out and stick it up somewhere you can see it every day.
- *Revise your bucket list* - your list of things to do or achieve before you make your exit from this world. Revise it at the beginning of every year and commit to ticking a couple off.
- *Have a pj day* - have one day when you get to sleep in, have breakfast in bed, read, lounge on the couch and order take out in the evening - without getting out of your pyjamas.

Begin with just one ritual as soon as you can and start taking care of yourself. Make sure you notice how you feel and how it changes you. Knowing that you are intentionally taking time out for yourself will guarantee a smoother and more balanced journey through life.

ॐ **Action:** Create a list of non-negotiable rituals for the morning and evening. Start your first ritual today.

ॐ **Song:** Cheap Thrills - Sia

by Lenore Pearson

Chapter 22
Ship Maintenance

You'll never change your life until you change something you do daily. The secret of your success is found in your daily routine.
~ John C. Maxwell

Ship maintenance is a fundamental component of any voyage. Just because you have returned to port doesn't mean that the hard work is over, if anything the maintenance of your ship is now more crucial than ever. Efficient maintenance prolongs the life of your ship, ensures equipment and machinery are updated and leads to smoother sailing in the future.

This includes tasks such as careening (turning the ship on its side), cleaning, caulking (sealing joints against leakage), repairing, oiling the decks and waxing and polishing the exterior for 'shininess'. A ship also needs its engine maintained so it has enough power to progress to the next destination.

Consider your health and wellness as the engine room of your ship. If you stop working, everything else stops working too. If you don't have enough fuel or the joints are sticking, it will slow your progress. Just like an engine needs constant TLC, so does your health and wellness. If you are working in top shape, then any journey is quicker and smoother regardless of the challenges along the way. When you focus on yourself in this way, this becomes your 'life maintenance'.

Your life maintenance involves three areas: your mind, your body and your soul. Once you recognise that true health and wellness involves working on all three aspects, you'll never view life quite the same again. If even only one area is not as it should be, you can never feel your best. You might be committed to the gym and have an incredible physique, but your mind may be at the point of exhaustion and your soul adrift as you have undertaken the single-minded pursuit of your physical goal. The aim here would be to scale back your gym time a bit and start working on positive thinking and developing a deeper sense of peace and understanding in a soulful or spiritual way. This is 'holistic' health. You can begin with any of those three areas but be sure to include all of them to complete your sense of wholeness.

Once you have begun your path to holistic health and wellness, you need to start a program of maintenance. In the nautical world there are three types of maintenance schedules for a ship:

- Preventive maintenance
- Corrective maintenance
- Condition maintenance

With this in mind, here is a maintenance schedule for you to consider:

Preventive maintenance
This is scheduled maintenance to prevent things from going wrong. Ideally this ought to be done daily.

Gratitude - if you are able to open your eyes every morning and take a big deep breath then you have a lot to be grateful for. You may be familiar with the practice of keeping a gratitude journal, where you record three things in your day that you are grateful for, but are you familiar with the Japanese gratitude practice of Naikan?

This is a practice of self-reflection and translated it means looking inside or introspection. It broadens your view of reality. This type of gratitude practice is based on asking three questions:
- What have I received from people in my life?
- What have I given to people in my life?
- What troubles and difficulties have I caused people in my life?

Self Ashored

The last question is a tricky one because it is easy to recall troubles and difficulties people have caused you but how easy is it to call to mind what you have caused others? By implementing this practice, you begin to realise you've been given far more than you can ever possibly repay. This is not to riddle yourself with guilt, but to allow you to become more conscious of how fortunate you are and how indebted you are to others for what you have been given throughout your life. Expressing gratitude switches the pathways in your brain from negative to positive and releases happy hormones such as oxytocin; it also helps you focus on what is already good in your life. Practicing gratitude everyday turns what you have into enough rather than always looking for more. It is soul work at its finest.

Meditate - this should come as no surprise as it's not the first time it's been mentioned in this book. Meditation teaches you that your mind and thoughts don't control you; you control your mind and thoughts. Thinking is what your mind does, that's its job, but those thoughts have no significance unless you give meaning to them. In her bestselling book *You Can Heal Your Life*, Louise Hay poses a very interesting way of looking at meditation, by recommending you sit and ask yourself, 'What do I need to know today?' If we gain control of our unhelpful thoughts then we are boosting our ability to deal with the next challenge that comes along.

Affirmations – again, no surprises here. Create your own or treat yourself to a beautifully illustrated box of cards. I adore my Gabrielle Bernstein *The Universe Has Your Back* affirmation deck, from which I pull a card every morning and whatever I pick is my affirmation for the day. This is another way to make your thoughts boost your wellbeing rather than detract from it.

Intention - begin your day by setting an intention. This gives your day more clarity and direction. Think of it as one of the keys on your map, without it it's like setting off on a voyage and not knowing where you're headed. And when you accomplish it you'll gain that wonderful feeling of achievement.

Ten pages - I am a self-professed bibliophile. I keep buying books before I finish reading the fifty that are already on my bedside table. If you're like me, a great way to help this along is to take Jeff Olsen's advice in *The Slight Edge:* to read ten pages of a book every day. What you feed your mind is just as important as what you feed your body, so to get maximum benefit out of your reading time, read life-altering material (I have included an awesome list of books in the resources section at the end of this book). Few of us feel as if we really have time to read, but I bet you could find time for just ten pages.

Listen - tune into quality content from some of your favourite speakers through a podcast. Listening to one inspiring podcast a day is a no-cost, time efficient and beneficial way to improve personal development (I have included some of my favourites in the resources section). This is a great way of learning anytime, anywhere. Listening to a podcast is a great way to leverage time spent in the car, in a waiting room, on public transport, or while you exercise.

Exercise - set goals for better physical health. It reduces the risk of cardiovascular disease, diabetes, cancer and obesity and is also invaluable for mental health. I make no secret of the fact that I'm not a gym person; I tried it, thought I was badass for turning up and getting on the treadmill for ten minutes in my new activewear, didn't stick with it because I had zero accountability, but then I found yoga. Yoga was much more my style and pace and the benefits of doing as little as twenty minutes a day were instantly noticeable. Better still, I could do it in the comfort of my own home. When it comes to exercise it's about finding what works for you, what you enjoy and consistency.

by Lenore Pearson

Clean Eating - you need to be conscious of what you are feeding your body. A good rule to follow is to eat food in as natural state as possible. The more food is added to or processed, the lower the nutritional value and the greater the chance of absorbing chemicals and additives. I used to knock my mum terribly for standing in the shopping aisle and reading packet labels. That was until I became a mum myself and it wasn't just about what I was consuming but what my children were consuming too - scary! It's not about the latest dieting fad; it's about making educated choices.

Switch off - I cannot stress this enough. In an age where it is a necessity to be switched on and plugged in, for your own mental health and wellness, allocate an hour each day to switching off. If you are brave enough, go one step further and give yourself a technology free day once a week. Disconnect to reconnect with yourself and other people.

Corrective maintenance
Corrective maintenance is carried out when things break down. It could be a breakdown in communication, breakdown of a relationship or breakdown of the mind and body. This is where medical practitioners, coaches, counsellors, help lines and organisations all play a part. The biggest wave you need to jump over when it comes to seeking out help is

your own belief that you'll muddle through on your own. The best way to look at it is 'course correcting' (more on this in Chapter 24), you've veered off course and you just need someone to help you find the best way to get back on track. It's not a sign of weakness to get help.

Condition maintenance

Condition maintenance is a way of checking-in to see what state of repair each part of your life is in. If something is not right you can begin corrective maintenance, or if you sense something is on the horizon you can embark on preventive maintenance instead. Here are some essential questions to ask yourself as part of your conditioning:

- How do I feel in this moment?
- What mindset am I employing each day?
- Am I putting enough effort into my relationships?
- What do I need to do to physically and mentally feel my best?
- What do I need to heal?
- Am I living a life authentic to me?

Another component of condition maintenance is personal development. This is about investing in yourself and expanding your knowledge and awareness. It is all about having a growth mindset, where you never stop learning. Be open to opportunities to hear your favourite motivational speakers live, attend conferences or seminars two to three times a year in your field of expertise or purely for interest. I have heard the Dalai Lama and Eckhart Tolle (*The Power of Now*) speak in Sydney and Mel Robbins (*The 5 Second Rule*) speak in Las Vegas and after each I walked away that little bit taller and more inspired.

In my opinion one of the best forms of condition maintenance is travel. If anything is going to put your life into perspective it's travelling to foreign lands, immersing yourself in the culture and ultimately realising that the world is abundant with good people. Once a year, go somewhere you've never been. You don't necessarily have to spend thousands of dollars on an overseas trip; you can just as easily try being a tourist in your own city. Paulo Coelho says, 'travel is never a matter of money but of courage'. One of the best things I have done for myself to date is travel on my own: firstly because it was such an important part of my healing journey but secondly because travel stirs up fears for many of us. We fear the unknown and the things we have never experienced before, we watch the news and see unrest and poverty and we wonder about our own safety travelling in a foreign land not knowing the language. Yet travelling on my own opened my eyes to how truly exquisite the world is and every moment was worth the risk.

If you remember to ask yourself the following three questions every day, you can't go far wrong with life maintenance:
- What am I doing for my mind?
- What am I doing for my body?
- What am I doing for my soul?

ॐ **Action:** Devise your own maintenance schedule. List daily, monthly and yearly tasks and add them to your calendar.

ॐ **Song:** Everybody's Free (To Wear Sunscreen) - Baz Luhrmann

by Lenore Pearson

Chapter 23
Make Ship Happen

I like things to happen; and if they don't happen, I like to make them happen.
~ Winston Churchill

Having put a solid maintenance schedule in place, the only other thing left for you to do is get some clarity on where to go from here and then make ship happen. At this point you'll find that you're one of three types of people: someone who makes things happen, someone who watches things happen or someone who constantly wonders what the hell happened. If you are in the latter two categories you have some work to do if you are ever going to make progress to where you're headed. You need to become someone who makes things happen more consistently.

Seneca the Younger wrote, 'No wind blows in favour of a ship without direction'. How are things ever going to work out if you don't know where you're headed? This is where you need a flock of 'SEA-goals' to head you up in the right direction. SEA stands for strategy, execution and assessment. Using this framework is an effective way to start making ship happen. You set your vision, decide, act and then assess your progress towards your goal.

Strategy

Strategy is all about your plan of attack, so get up to the crow's nest of your ship with your telescope and have a look around. You need vision. To do this, notice all the opportunities and possible destinations laid out before you and begin to home in on one. While you're up there, you also need to get a sense of where you are now in the expanse of the ocean. Once you have done this, you'll be able to pinpoint your goal with precision and you can start to chart a course. Your course is your strategy and how you're going to get there. You then begin to plan your steps along the way with as much clarity as you can.

I once read that you should never have a plan B because it means you don't wholeheartedly believe that your plan A will work. As someone who struggles with anxiety, always having a plan B seemed like a great idea. It was my safety net and so if plan A didn't work then there was something in place to catch me should I fall. What I realised was that by always having a plan B, I was basically waiting for plan A to fail. More often than not it became a self-fulfilling prophecy. If you believe in something so strongly, put your time and energy into committing 100% to it rather than thinking too far ahead. Instead, start your journey and focus solely on plan A and believe that you will know how to adjust if you get thrown off course.

As you plan your strategy, you can build in provisions to keep you going. One important provision is accountability. By having a way of keeping yourself accountable, you have a way to stay on track. This might come in the form of a shipmate who can take the journey with you, or coach you along the way. Alternatively, you might consider making good use of social media or a blog to log your journey so that your followers can hold you accountable to your goal.

Execution
The first step is often the hardest. When you know you need to make something happen it is all too easy to let doubt paralyse you. You can begin to fight away this doubt by igniting your resolve. This is the unwavering determination that you will reach your goal no matter what. No matter how long it takes and no matter how many times the little voice in your head tells you to quit, you will succeed.

Once you have ignited your resolve, you can work out your first step. Momentum is never gained by standing still. Analyse your situation to determine one thing you can do right now and then do it. Then make plans for your next step and then the one after that and before you know it, you'll be on your way.

A ship's speed is measured in knots. This term came from counting the number of knots in a length of rope that unspooled from a ship as it moved. Taking small steps is like the knots in that rope. You start with the very first one and then as you gain speed and momentum, the knots come more quickly. However, you may find the need to pause and ask for help. This is especially important when you don't know where to go next, or maybe you do know but the next step is just out of reach of your strength, capability, or know-how. This is when you call on your rowing team. If you've been able to get some trusted friends on board your ship, you'll have people to turn to when things get tough. Even if they can't help directly, they may be able to point you in the right direction. Remember that there are always options but only you know the right option for you. Make sure your decision making comes from your authentic self or you may come to regret the choices you make down the track.

It is important to realise that making ship happen doesn't necessarily have to come with sacrifice and struggle. These things may be part of the journey but how things turn out is directly related to how you respond to the challenges you encounter. If fear grips

by Lenore Pearson

you or you allow the tough times to slow you down, you face the danger of being demoted from captain to crew member on your own ship at the mercy of the waves. Instead you need to own the role like a badass. Grab hold of life and make a difference. Be careful though, you may be guilted by those around you into becoming one of the crew again, but you need to let go of the guilt and figure out who you really are and what you really want. Never hold back for fear of outshining someone else, being different or doing the unexpected, no matter what anyone says. Captain your own ship.

Assessment
This aspect of your SEA-goals is perhaps the most important. So important, in fact, that the entire next chapter is devoted to it. Assessment is how you gauge your progress. It helps you stay on course. When you begin to journey toward your goal, you need to build in checkpoints along the way that provide an indication of what your journey should look like at certain stages. Be prepared to be flexible and review your checkpoints from time to time or as conditions on your voyage change.

Ultimately, making ship happen can be, all at once, the most exhilarating and the most frightening experience you can have. However, with a little thinking, preparation, vision, strategy and the right kind of execution you can change your life. Once you set your heart on something and decide to make it happen, you ultimately become unstoppable.

Don't stand still waiting for life to happen, make it happen.

ॐ **Action**: Write down one thing you wish to achieve, share it with someone you trust that can hold you accountable and then take the first step towards achieving it.

ॐ **Song**: Unstoppable - Sia

Chapter 24
Course Correct

Failure is just information and an opportunity to change your course.
~Oprah Winfrey

You now possess a 'Life Kit' of skills and tools you can utilise throughout your voyage. However, even the most well equipped captain with the best laid out plans cannot guarantee a free pass on making mistakes and potential failure. What if some things just don't work out the way you had planned?

From time to time on your journey, you may find your ship off course, becalmed or even having sprung a leak. You may have taken a step in the wrong direction or even landed yourself in troubled waters. Take a moment to see if you can fix the situation yourself, or if you can't, find a life raft. A life raft is a temporary measure, something to get you out of trouble in the short term. It's not big enough to get you where you're going but it will certainly help you stay afloat.

When my husband changed careers from a teacher to a real estate agent it was a big risk. He took the right steps to change his course and suddenly found himself quitting his steady pay cheque and exchanging it for unreliable commission payments. After the first couple of commissions were spent, the money stopped but the bills didn't. He had sprung a leak. He took steps to fix it with the help of his boss, but he was sinking fast. What he needed was a life raft. It came in the form of a part-time job making pizzas. He now had just enough money coming in to cover expenses in between commissions and the few hours he spent of an evening earning some extra money didn't affect his ability to perform his main job. He wasn't afraid of plunging in and trying something new. He trusted in his ability to make good plans even if things went wrong.

Using a life raft is just one way of coping when things go wrong. My husband needed a temporary solution when he hit a rough patch. But this isn't quite the same as when you know that you've made a mistake. What if my husband had discovered that he couldn't sell real estate? What if the company he signed up for folded, leaving him high and dry? A life raft would not have been sufficient. He would have needed to course correct to find a way of making good his mistake.

I think there is a very clear distinction between making a mistake and failing at something. Mistakes come about from being misguided due to a lack of the

by Lenore Pearson

relevant information required to make an educated decision. It is an indication that there is still room for growth and more information is needed to avoid making the same mistake again. Failure on the other hand, is a choice to keep making wrong decisions without learning from them.

Failure is a completely internal process; it is all in how you perceive it. If you let failure dictate the rest of your course, the outcome can be a little like the Bermuda Triangle. You get so caught up in the fact you made a mistake that you frighten the ship out of yourself. You become so paralysed by the thought of getting back out there and trying again that you often end up being stuck in a vicious cycle and never being able to return to your journey. If you're not careful your fear of failure will be your greatest downfall, because you become so focussed on the end product that you miss the process. The longer you sit with your failure, the more fear sets in and prevents you from getting back on your ship and setting sail once again. Just because you put all your strength into the process of rebuilding your ship once before, doesn't mean you can't do it again, this time with more fuel to keep you going towards a new horizon. Your new knowledge, hard-won through your mistakes is your fuel. Add it to the energy supply and make it work for you, not against you. Every mistake has a lesson; it's a building block.

Self Ashored

The only time you can ever treat something as a failure is if you didn't learn and grow from it.

Let's assume for a moment that my husband's career change was a mistake, that he wasn't cut out for sales work. It would have been a failure had he switched agencies to see if the grass was greener somewhere else. It would have been a failure had he picked up more shifts making pizzas, something he didn't have a passion for. Neither of these would have long term solutions. He would have circled back to discovering that he couldn't do the job he had signed up for, repeating the failure and not learning from the mistake. Had he returned to teaching, taken extra courses in sales, or found a way to marry his teaching skills with his passion for real estate, then any of these would have been much more successful course corrections.

One of the things I love most about my job is that I am in a unique position where I get to see people in a way that they can't yet see themselves. One of my clients was a talented figure skater with a promising career ahead of her until injury took her out of the game. During our sessions, it came to light that she regretted not being able to stick with skating long enough to earn her way to the Olympics. She felt that she had failed, not only in her eyes but those around her. What she hadn't realised was that she had course corrected by pursuing a career path in the health and wellness industry. There was no way she could have continued skating. To stick with it would have ended in more injury and genuine failure. She needed to realise that her destination had changed. She had already taken the necessary steps to course correct, she just hadn't realised that her 'Olympic Moment' was potentially going to come in some other way. It would have been very easy for her to get stuck in the thought that she had failed but she had already learnt the lesson she needed to move on. Sometimes all you need is to reboot your GPS, your internal tracking device. You need to discover that the right path often lies in a completely different direction, but sooner or later you will arrive back on track at the same destination.

Indications you need a course correction

- ***The fuel tank is empty*** - you physically feel in your body that something isn't right. You struggle to get out of bed in the morning; you can't get through the day without taking a nap. Your health or mood suffers.
- ***Bad reception*** - you are unhappy in a relationship. Often this happens because the lines of communication are distorted, throwing compromise and understanding overboard.

- *A tidal wave is about to hit* - something is about to give, you are giving too much of your time and energy to the wrong things. If you keep headed down this path then it could become a natural disaster.
- *The Siren's call is getting louder* - your inner mean voice is resurfacing, leading to a comparison war with other people and a pang of jealousy when you see other people succeed.
- *You have ventured into shark-infested waters* - you dread going to work each morning for fear of entering the shark's tank. You are surrounded by people who pull you down instead of raise you up.
- *Your GPS signal is weak* - you know the direction you are heading in is not the right one for you because you have a constant longing for something more. You just don't know what it is yet.

No one is immune to mistake making. You may have dated the wrong people, kissed a few toads before you got the prince, spent years in a thankless job, made poor investment choices, dropped out of university or lost your ship at your best friend. My advice is to own it. Accept your mistake for what it is but don't let it colour the rest of your life. Course correcting is not giving up, it's giving in to something you know in your

by Lenore Pearson

gut is better for you. In the same way, you are the only one who can define your failure; you are also the only one who can define your success.

Imagine if your mistakes could become your successes? It has been said that Elvis was told he couldn't sing, that Michael Jordan was cut from his high school basketball team and that it took thirty attempts for Stephen King to have his first novel published. How will you ever know what you are capable of if you don't get back on your ship? Learn from your mistakes, correct your course and get back out there.

ॐ **Action:** Identify one of your biggest mistakes. What lesson did you learn? What changes have you made in your life because of it?

ॐ **Song:** You Learn - Alanis Morissette

Chapter 25
Ripples

Individually, we are one drop. Together, we are an ocean.
~ Ryunosuke Satoro

When you contemplate your existence in this world, you might feel like a drop in the ocean, but when the water is calm, have you ever noticed the ripple effect one drop in the ocean can make?

The only thing as important as what you do for yourself is what you do for other people. Take everything you have learnt about yourself, what you have worked on internally, and prepare to make an impact externally. If you are sitting there thinking that you couldn't possibly make a difference in someone else's life, let alone the entire world, you couldn't be more wrong.

When I was young, I would love to throw pebbles into still water so I could watch the ripples get bigger and bigger as they moved out. I would turn it into a game and count to see how many rings I could create and try to beat my score every time. As I got older, I came to learn that what created those ripples was energy and

by Lenore Pearson

that the size of the pebble and the force with which I threw it affected how many ripples were created and how far they travelled.

You are a pebble in the ocean of life. Your thoughts and actions are what create the ripples that move outward. Everything you say and every action you take does not just affect you, it affects everyone around you, sometimes without you knowing just how much. How people react to that, in turn, affects others. Your impact on the world is far greater than you could ever imagine.

You get to decide with what energy, force and intent you impact the world - do you play small, creating a little splash with smaller ripples or do you play big, using your strength, determination and positive energy to produce ripples that have the potential to radiate out into the world long after you are gone?

It wasn't until I became a mum that I realised just how powerful my words and actions were. There is a beautiful little reserve at the end of our street with a winding path that leads down to a little bridge over a gently running stream. My kids love to take a walk down there and find rocks to throw in the water. My husband decided to give me a bit of relief one day to get some writing done and took the younger two for a walk to the bridge. When they arrived home, my son Lucas walked in and said, 'Mum don't get angry, but I fell in the water', and then handed me his sopping-wet *good* going-out shoes! I was just about to embark on a sensational rant about how you don't wear your good shoes down to the stream and you need to be more careful and what were you doing so close to the water, when he stopped me and said, 'Mum, I was just doing what you taught me to do, to create ripples in the water!' My next choice of words either had the power to crush him or raise him up. I decided that one day I was going to be able to remind him just how powerful his words were and I continued to explain to him the deeper meaning behind creating ripples. To this day he still reminds me of this conversation.

There are many ways to be impactful. Here are six I know work every single time:

How to be impactful

- ***Pay it forward*** - when someone shows you kindness, pay it forward by showing someone else kindness. It is a common belief that impact means large scale; never underestimate the difference a small gesture or smile can make to someone's day. This sort of gesture can be infectious as one person passes it on to the next.

by Lenore Pearson

- *Be authentic* - if you want to change the world, start with yourself. Stop comparing yourself to what other people have done with their life and concentrate on doing you. No one else can bring to this world what you have to offer, because no one else is you. Your power comes from your uniqueness.
- *Pick one* - there are so many worthy and deserving causes and organisations to support but don't spread yourself too thin. Choose one that really resonates with you and dedicate your time or money to bringing awareness to their work.
- *Don't be afraid to be vulnerable* - when you raise your hand and say, 'me too' or, 'I need help', you allow yourself to be seen and heard in a way others are afraid to. By doing this you give permission for others to do the same. Vulnerability creates trust and understanding. These two qualities are what allow groups of all kinds to bond together and work toward a common purpose.
- *Approach to life* - with everything in life, approach it with love, compassion and patience. It is absolutely true that what you put out you get back. It really is that simple. Positive ripples may not be seen straight away but I promise you, with those three qualities, the far-reaching

effects will be felt for years to come. You cannot fail to have an impact.
- *Intention* - this is possibly the most important. People argue that they give so much of themselves to others. They give their time, they give their money, they always offer to do things and yet they complain that they get nothing in return. My question is what is your intention behind giving? Are you looking to amplify the life of someone else or are you doing it for what you'll get out of it? Never do anything with the intent of expecting repayment; you will be disappointed every single time and, worse still, this kind of intent stunts your ripples. The intent behind your words and actions is the energy that will either create ever-emanating ripples of positivity that multiplies long after you're gone or create a foamy wash of negativity that erases any trace of what little impact you may have had. Your intention needs to be so much bigger than what you want to get out of it. You may never discover the impact your life has on another and how they use it to impact someone else but this doesn't diminish your impact. Do it anyway.

Your life is already surprisingly impactful. This is regardless of whether you believe it or not. What you

by Lenore Pearson

do, what you say, what you don't do and what you don't say all matters. Never doubt that you can change the world. You may never come to know the impact, that part of your story still lies unwritten in the future, but don't let that stop you from doing it anyway. Don't be the reason someone falls short, be the reason they get to leave their own ripples in this world. The impact and change you make is entirely up to you.

You are the most powerful person you know.

ॐ **Action:** Go for a walk and find yourself a beautiful pebble. Keep it as a reminder of all the positive ripples you will create.

ॐ **Song:** Unwritten - Natasha Bedingfield

Chapter 26
Buried Treasure

There is no passion to be found playing small – in settling for a life that is less than the one you are capable of living.
~ Nelson Mandela

You have been on quite the journey.

My intention for this book was for you to learn who you really are and for the way you saw yourself at the beginning to be very different to how you see yourself now. In doing so, it was my hope for you to use this to forge an unbreakable bond with yourself so that you are always connected to your true authentic self.

Believe me when I tell you that every moment and experience that has brought you to this point in your life has been for a purpose. These experiences, both good and bad, have given you the best opportunity to get to know who you really are. Without moments of shipwreck or drowning, you won't learn how to rebuild and find the courage to start again with the desire of something better. Without that courage and desire, you may never 'seas the day' and set off for new horizons. Those new horizons will force you to learn

by Lenore Pearson

new skills and move out of the safety of your harbour where new challenges are met. Those challenges are sent to test you and mask themselves as a perfect storm or a sea full of creatures with a hidden sting or bite. Yet without them, you never get to know the beauty of other people, the importance of protecting your energy and the power of your intuition.

It is only through all this that you come to know who you really are, what you stand for, the kinds of people you want to take along with you, how to maintain what you have learnt, what to do if you get thrown off course and ultimately how to create impact in the lives of others.

Every great voyage in history began with the intention of finding something: new land, new animals, or even new people. Each one of these is a unique version of someone's buried treasure. But your buried treasure was not something you had to embark on an epic voyage for and it wasn't something you lost or never possessed, for it has resided in you all along. You just forgot or never knew how to access it.

There is a scene at the end of the movie *The Wizard of Oz*, where Dorothy is ready to leave the Emerald City and return home to Kansas, and she asks Glinda the Good Witch for help. As Glinda points to Dorothy's

Self Ashored

ruby slippers, she makes it known to Dorothy that she didn't need her help because she had the power to return home all along. Just like Dorothy, you've had the power all along. No book is going to tell you exactly how to be you, no amount of looking externally will bring you any closer to what already resides within you and you didn't really need me to come along on your voyage, you just needed me to hold up the mirror.

In many ways writing this book saved my own life; I was in danger of doing all the things I tell people not to do. This book became the mirror I needed so I could get really clear on how I wanted to be seen in the world.

Your treasure is not wealth, property or even a new discovery. Instead it is the very thing that has been buried far within the depths of your being for far too long. It is your voice. I'm not talking about the tone or volume of your voice; I am talking about the voice that is the echo of your soul. Your voice is a metaphor for what makes you you, it represents your energy in the world. Your voice is your way of articulating your character. Like your fingerprint, no one else in the whole world has your voice. It is the one thing that can never be taken from you for even those that can't speak have a voice. Your voice is the single most important force on your voyage. It is what catches in the sails and

by Lenore Pearson

propels you forward to living a life of fulfilment, rich with possibility.

The moment you access your voice is the moment you own your life so that you can live authentically, being true to your purpose. I can't tell you how to use your voice, that is something you need to work out for yourself, but never underestimate its power once you have done the required reflection to access it. If you ever feel like someone else's lies overshadow your truth or you don't like the conversation going on around you, change it. One of the things that break my heart the most is watching people hide who they really are; people who are afraid to raise their voice and be heard, who live a life less than they are capable of living. Never use your voice to drown out the voices of others. Raise it in such a way that you give those around you a reason to want to raise theirs and be heard in a way that will change lives for the better.

Nowadays everyone is so intent on getting to where they're going as fast as they can…it's BS! My dad always used to say, 'The last shall be first'. You move too fast, you miss the process of learning and growing; you will tread on a lot of people and find that at the top it gets lonely unless you remember to build people up and bring them with you. Stop thinking that you have to have it all figured out, you're not supposed to. You

Self Ashored

just need to work out how to navigate life as it unfolds. Stop thinking that your life is not where you thought it would be by this stage. Instead, celebrate it for all that it is because the way in which you have journeyed, if you have lived authentically, may have averted some pretty big disasters further ahead. Stop telling people the opposite of what you really want, you're not fooling anyone but yourself, so be honest and use your voice; get very clear on your true intentions and then start taking steps to get them.

Please, please stop comparing yourself to everyone else. What appears to you as a person 'living the dream life' is only a paragraph in a chapter of the whole story of their life. You don't see their daily struggle to raise a family or even start one, you don't see $17 in a bank account that needs to last until the next pay day, you aren't hearing the internal thoughts of self-doubt and unworthiness and you aren't seeing the millions of goals that haven't been met. What you *are* seeing is someone who intentionally chooses to be happy despite the challenges.

I don't care if you are five, fifty-five or a hundred and five, it's never too early or late to be who you want to be. There is no perfect time or age; if someone makes you believe otherwise then they don't deserve a place on your ship. The only restrictions in your life are the ones you place on yourself. Don't make the mistake of pinning your worth on what other people think and say, whether they are proud of you or whether they are interested enough to ask what you're doing or how you're really going. You and you alone determine your worth.

You need to realise that you are somebody worthwhile already. Start acting like you are meant to be here and the confidence will follow. Who you were in the past does not define who you are now and who you are now is only preparing you for who you will become. That 'now' person needs you to give them permission to shine and be seen and heard the way I know you were born to do.

So use your voice and step up.

Step up to the bow of your ship as its captain, summon all your courage and a new understanding of yourself and spread your arms wide to embrace the next part of your voyage.

Be *self-ashored*.

ॐ **Action:** For the love of all that is good in this world, don't be afraid to shine. Step up and show the world what you're made of. Be someone else's lighthouse, gently guiding them to their destination. Pick one thing to change now so that you shine.

ॐ **Song:** Hall of Fame - The Script

by Lenore Pearson

Glossary of Terms

Bibliophile - a person who collects or has a great love of books.
Black Death plague - one of the most devastating pandemics in history that resulted in an estimated 75 - 200 million deaths during the 14th century.
Bow - the front end of a ship.
Bulkheads - separate compartments inside a ship.
Bunkering - refilling fuel containers on a ship.
Careening - to turn a ship on its side for cleaning.
Caulking - use of a waterproof sealant for repairs on a ship.
Crow's Nest - a platform fixed at the masthead of a ship as a place to look out.
Dead weight - the total weight of cargo, stores, etc. which a ship carries.
Egocentric - thinking only of oneself without regard for the feelings of others.
Fight or Flight - the instinctive physiological response to a threatening situation, which prepares a person to either fight the threat or run from it.
Figurehead - a carving of a bust or full-length figure, set at the prow of an old-fashioned sailing ship.
GPS - Global Positioning System - a satellite based navigation system.
Harbour pilot - a sailor who maneuvers ships through

dangerous or congested waters, such as harbours or river mouths.
Hull - the main body of a ship.
Keel - the lengthwise timber or steel structure along the base of a ship, supporting the framework.
Keel Over - when a ship tilts so far to one side that it can't recover. It capsizes.
Kraken - an enormous mythical sea monster said to appear off the coast of Norway.
Law of Attraction - the belief that by focusing on positive or negative thoughts, people can bring positive or negative experiences into their life.
Loving Kindness Meditation - a method of developing compassion first for yourself, second for someone you are closely connected with, third for someone you feel neutral about, fourth for someone you don't like or have difficulty connecting with and lastly for everyone.
Negativity Bias - the brain's bias for focusing on things of a more negative nature rather than positive, even if the positives in a situation outweighs the negative.
Port of Call - a place where a ship stops on a voyage.
Poseidon - The Greek god of the sea often depicted with a trident in his hand. The Roman equivalent is Neptune.
Prow - the pointed front part of a ship.
Ritual - A religious or solemn ceremony consisting of a series of actions performed according to a prescribed order.

by Lenore Pearson

Sea Dog - an old or experienced sailor.
Sea Legs - a person's ability to keep their balance and not feel seasick when on board a moving ship.
Sea Trial - the testing phase of a ship, usually the last stage of construction.
Self Ashored – a firm belief in one's own abilities or character.
Seven Seas - all the oceans of the world (conventionally listed as the Arctic, Antarctic, North Pacific, South Pacific, North Atlantic, South Atlantic, and Indian Oceans).
Shamanic - relating to the beliefs and practices associated with a shaman.
Shark Spotter - someone who keeps watch for sharks and sounds a siren to alert unknowing swimmers.
Shipwright - a shipbuilder.
Siren - a mythical woman or winged creature whose singing lured unwary sailors on to rocks.
Stern - the rearmost part of a ship.
Stores - supplies of equipment and food kept for use by crew on a ship.
Subconscious Mind - the part of the mind of which one is not fully aware but which influences one's actions and feelings.
Unstoppable - impossible to stop or prevent; also the name of Bethany Hamilton and Adam Dirks's book for children, *Unstoppable Me*.

Source: English Oxford Living Dictionaries

The Self Ashored Playlist

- This Is Me - Keala Settle
- Changing Tides - The Fray
- Feeling A Moment - Feeder
- Raise Your Glass - Pink
- Never Give Up - Sia
- Dare You to Move - Switchfoot
- Free to Be Me - Francesca Battistelli
- Brand New Day - Alex Lloyd
- How Far I'll Go - Alessia Cara
- Dancing in The Storm - Boom Crash Opera
- Fight Song - Rachel Platten
- Going Under - Evanescence
- Titanium - David Guetta feat. Sia
- Roar - Katy Perry
- Change Your Life - Little Mix
- The Great Escape - Pink
- I Don't Want to Be - Gavin DeGraw
- Suddenly I See - KT Tunstall
- St Elmo's Fire (Man in Motion) - John Parr
- Pure Shores - All Saints
- Stand by You - Rachel Platten
- Cheap Thrills - Sia
- Everybody's Free (To Wear Sunscreen) - Baz Luhrmann
- Unstoppable - Sia

by Lenore Pearson

- You Learn - Alanis Morissette
- Unwritten - Natasha Bedingfield
- Hall of Fame - The Script

Visit my website www.lenorepearson.com for links to The Self Ashored Spotify and YouTube playlists plus bonus material.

Recommended Resources

BOOKS
- *The Universe Has Your Back* - Gabrielle Bernstein
- *Judgement Detox* - Gabrielle Bernstein
- *Daring Greatly* - Brene Brown
- *The Gifts of Imperfection* - Brene Brown
- *The Secret* - Rhonda Byrne
- *The Art of Happiness* - HH the Dalai Lama
- *The Miracle Morning* - Hal Elrod
- *Man's Search for Meaning* - Viktor Frankl
- *Big Magic* - Elizabeth Gilbert
- *Tribes* - Seth Godin
- *You Can Heal Your Life* - Louise Hay
- *Meditation as Medicine* - Dharma Singh Khalsa
- *The Life Changing Magic of Not Giving a F**k* - Sarah Knight
- *Biology of Belief* - Dr Bruce Lipton
- *Failing Forward* - John C. Maxwell
- *The Empath's Survival Guide* – Judith Orloff
- *Mind Over Medicine* - Dr Lissa Rankin
- *The 5 Second Rule* - Mel Robbins
- *The Four Agreements* - Don Miguel Ruiz
- *Oh The Places You'll Go* - Dr. Seuss
- *You Are A Badass* - Jen Sincero
- *First We Make The Beast Beautiful* - Sarah Wilson

by Lenore Pearson

PODCASTS
- Happier with Gretchen Rubin
- Happy Mama Movement with Amy Taylor - Kabbaz
- Magic Lessons with Elizabeth Gilbert
- Oprah's Super Soul Conversations
- The Mindful Kind
- The Robin Sharma Mastery Sessions
- The Thrive Global Podcast with Arianna Huffington
- Village Mama
- Wanderlust Speakeasy
- Wellness Women Radio
- Your Dream Life with Kristina Karlsson

TED TALKS
- Sparks: How Youth Thrive - Dr. Peter Benson
- The Power of Vulnerability - Brene Brown
- Your Body Language May Shape Who You Are - Amy Cuddy
- The Gift and Power of Emotional Courage - Susan David
- The Surprising Science of Happiness - Dan Gilbert
- Your Elusive Creative Genius - Elizabeth Gilbert
- How To Know Your Life Purpose in 5 Minutes - Adam Leipzig

- How To Make Stress Your Friend - Kelly McGonigal
- Every Kid Needs a Champion - Rita Pierson
- The Shocking Truth About Your Health - Dr Lissa Rankin
- My Year of Saying Yes to Everything - Shonda Rimes
- How to Stop Screwing Yourself Over - Mel Robbins
- How Great Leaders Inspire Action - Simon Sinek
- How The Worst Moments in Our Lives Make Us Who We Are - Andrew Solomon

WEBSITES
- www.lenorepearson.com - for bonus material
- Beyond Blue - https://www.beyondblue.org.au
- Black Dog Institute - https://www.blackdoginstitute.org.au
- Choose Real Campaign - http://chooserealcampaign.com
- Esteem Designz - http://esteemdesignz.com.au
- Goalcast - www.goalcast.com
- Life Line - https://www.lifeline.org.au
- Man Up - http://manup.org.au
- Men's Line - https://mensline.org.au
- PANDA - Perinatal Anxiety and Depression Australia - www.panda.org.au

- TED Talks - www.ted.com

YOU TUBE CLIPS

- The Incomparable Malala Yousafzai – The Ellen Show
- Before You Judge - Gabrielle Bernstein
- Dealing With and Overcoming Loss - Jack Canfield
- How to Create a Vision Board - Jack Canfield
- How to Deal with Negative Self Talk - Jack Canfield
- How to Overcome the Fears You Create - Jack Canfield
- The Present - short animation by Jacob Frey
- The Biology of Belief - Dr Bruce Lipton
- Make Your Bed - Admiral William McRaven | Goalcast
- Mind Over Medicine - Dr Lissa Rankin
- How to Let Your Light Shine Bright - Lisa Nichols | Goalcast
- Set Your Life on Fire - Will Smith
- Failure - Will Smith

LOVING KINDNESS MEDITATION
1. Find a comfortable seated position. Close your eyes and spend a few minutes focussing on your breath.
2. Begin by sending loving kindness to yourself, repeating the following phrases in your mind:
- May I be peaceful and happy
- May I be well
- May I be safe
- May I be free from suffering
- May I live with joy
3. Now open the circle of loving kindness and bring to mind someone you love, repeating the following phrases in your mind:
- May you be peaceful and happy
- May you be well
- May you be safe
- May you be free from suffering
- May you live with joy
4. Now bring to mind a 'neutral' person, someone you might see regularly but not know well and repeat the above phrases.
5. If possible, bring to mind someone with whom you've had a difficult relationship with and repeat the above phrases.
6. Finish by sending loving kindness out to all beings and repeat the above phrases.

by Lenore Pearson

End your meditation practice with a beautiful universal word that means 'My soul honours your soul, I honour the place in you where the entire universe resides, I honour the light, love, truth, beauty and peace within you, because it is also within me. In sharing these things, we are united, we are the same, we are one'.

Namaste

Statistics

In the spirit of keeping it real, here's some statistics about the whole process!

Writing began on - 16th July 2018

- Cups of tea consumed - 450

- Packets of Mint Slice biscuits - 1…ok maybe 10

- Minutes spent staring at a blank screen - 9000

- Phone calls to my mum - 300

- Use of the 'F' word - too many to count

- Times I cried - at least once a day

- Times I made other people cry - at least once a day (but they probably asked for it)

- Songs I listened to on repeat on Spotify while writing my book - 30

by Lenore Pearson

- Blackmail attempts on my husband to edit my work - 150

- Times I let my children raid the pantry so I could get 10 mins of writing done in peace - 60

- Minutes wasted finding something interesting to read or watch on Facebook - 10,000

- Times I added 'Work on Book' to my To Do list after the fact so I could tick it off and look like I accomplished something that day - 150

- Months it took to write the book - 4.5

- Times I wanted to give up - every damn day!

- Times I thought this was worth every bit of emotion and energy - every damn day!

Acknowledgements

First and foremost, the biggest and most heartfelt thank you to Dallas; you are my 'Rare Starfish'. Thank you for popping into my life at a time when I wasn't ok, even though outwardly it seemed to those around me that I was. Thank you for giving me permission to use my voice and be proud of it at a time when I was slowly being scared into silence. Thank you for seeing the worth in my writing and asking me to share my story, for believing in me more than I believed in myself and for seeing me for me. I adore you.

To my mum Suzy, thank you for loving and trusting me wholeheartedly and never judging the way I chose to heal after we lost dad. Thank you for backing me one hundred percent with this book and for believing that it would make a difference. Thank you for telling me you are proud of me (even at my age I still need to know) but honestly it is me who is proud of you. You have been mother and father, grandmother and grandfather to your children and grandchildren and you have taken on each role with so much grace and strength, dad would be incredibly proud. You may not be able to see the beauty of the journey you have been on the last three years but trust me when I tell you, you are

by Lenore Pearson

shining in ways you never did before and your life is waiting for you to do great things. No mud, no lotus.

Dad, I know you were hovering over my shoulder as I wrote this book and that when I wanted to give up or couldn't find the words, your voice echoed in my ears 'Just keep going Len, you can do this'. Thank you for giving me the signs I needed to know I am exactly where I need to be and thank you for teaching me what it means to stay true to myself. Thank you for raising me to see the best in people but for also giving me the wisdom to know when to let people go. I miss you every single day; I hope I make you proud.

Thank you to my brother David and sister Debbie. I always took my role as the eldest very seriously and hoped that I could be a shining example of what an older sister should be, but over the last few years it is both of you that have taught me more about myself, about life and what it means to be a family. We certainly didn't get it right all the time and we have had our fair share of cracker arguments, but I am so honoured to have two very courageous siblings who have grown so much in spite of our loss. I hope you both see how far you have come.

To my godparents Mary and Sam, thank you for allowing me to ring you up in tears when I needed to and when I couldn't, for always letting me know you are there when I'm ready. I know dad would be so proud of the way you have both looked out for his family. I love you both.

My cousin Damian, you have some freakin serious talent! I am so thrilled to be able to share your gift with the world on the cover of my book. You did such an amazing job and I look forward to the day you publish your own art book.

I am so very grateful to Mitch for doing an incredible job of editing my book for me. Your excitement when I asked you to do this was the best reaction ever and I loved your words of encouragement along the way.

To Char, Lil, Tammi, Elle and Rich for taking the time to read, edit and write a blurb for my book. In the huge scheme of things, you have all only known me such a short time and yet you probably know me better than most. I chose you all because I trusted you with this book, but also because each of you have opened doors for me I didn't know existed and for that I am truly grateful.

Thank you, Scotty, for once again bravely allowing me to share your story with the world. I am so glad that our paths crossed at the horse races, I hope you now realise what a positive impact you had on my outlook on life.

Thank you to my clients for their belief and trust in me and for being brave enough to share their story and make a change.

To my gorgeous husband Stuart, babe I seriously don't know how you stayed married to me through all of this. Thank you for never giving up on me, especially when 'ship' hit the fan. Everything about our life is 'perfectly imperfect' but that's what makes us the best team ever. You and our three divine children light up my life in ways I never thought possible and through all of this I discovered the secret to a great marriage, to allow each other to shine when it's our time. You don't need to prove yourself to anyone because anyone worth having in your life knows how fiercely you protect your little family. You my darling are what every father and husband should aspire to be.

To my three beautiful children, I am not even close to being the mother I wanted to be but just know that I fight hard for you every single day.

My big boy Toby, my beautiful sensitive kid, thank you for being the head of my cheer squad. Thank you for always watching out for everybody else and being the third parent in our house. Your brother and sister may not realise it yet, but they have struck gold with you as their older brother. I know only too well that it isn't easy being the eldest and I also know what it is like to have certain expectations placed upon you that you feel you need to live up to. You are allowed to make mistakes, you are allowed to break the rules every now and again and you are allowed to speak up if you feel strongly enough about something. Thank you for letting me be an 'annoying' mum but always having a laugh with me. You are one super kid.

To my Lucas, sometimes I forget how young you are because you hit me with the most profound words. You remind me most of myself. A creative, big hearted, beautiful thinker who is often misunderstood because you march to the beat of your own drum. Thank you for teaching me how to be 'persuasive' in my book, for reading me my favourite Dr. Seuss book *Oh the Places You'll Go* when I felt stressed or sad and thank you for reminding me that it's ok to get overly excited about everything in life, a quality that many should adopt themselves. Don't ever let anyone change that my darling boy, you are perfect exactly as you are.

To my baby girl Audrey, you have the world's biggest voice and I love it. Sometimes when I tell you to lower your voice, I need to remind myself that you will raise your voice in ways that will change the world some day and to never extinguish that fire in your belly. Thank you for being my best friend.

Thank you to all the people who unwittingly gave me some of the best content for this book, the people who challenged me. You know what they say - never piss off an author because you may end up the subject of their next book!

Thank you to you, my reader, if you have made it this far. Just know that I see you, for all that you are and I hope in some small way I have helped you realise how amazing you truly are.

About the Author

Lenore is a Meditation Therapist, Holistic Counsellor and Life Coach. She is the founder of Artemis Meditation and Holistic Counselling based in Sydney, Australia. Lenore is an accomplished speaker and accredited practitioner in the Health and Wellbeing industry.

With extensive study in education, travel, health and wellness, she has built her experience both at home in Australia, and internationally.

by Lenore Pearson

Lenore's mission is to help people take control of their own lives. She is energetic, passionate and determined in her desire for people to not just feel healthy and balanced, but to feel whole.

At home, she is mum, focussing her love and energy on her three children and husband who are an endless source of inspiration and entertainment!

Lenore, my mum, is one of the bravest people I know. Not everyone can share their ideas and experiences with people like she does. I am so proud of her.

-Toby Pearson

Get in touch with Lenore via the following platforms:

- Website - www.lenorepearson.com
- Email - lenorepearsonholistic@gmail.com
- Facebook - @artemismhc
- Instagram - lenorepearson_holistic